It Happened In Series

It Happened In Atlanta

Remarkable Events That Shaped History

John McKay

Guilford, Connecticut

Project editor: Meredith Dias
Layout: Joanna Beyer
Map: Melissa Baker © Morris Book Publishing, LLC

McKay, John, 1959-
  It happened in Atlanta : remarkable events that shaped history / John McKay.
    p. cm.
  Includes bibliographical references and index.
  ISBN 978-0-7627-6439-6 (alk. paper)
  1. Atlanta (Ga.)—History—Anecdotes. 2. Atlanta (Ga.)—Biography—Anecdotes.
3. Atlanta (Ga.)—Social life and customs—Anecdotes. I. Title.
  F294.A84M35 2011
  975.8'231—dc22

                                                              2011016313

Printed in the United States of America
10 9 8 7 6 5 4 3 2 1

CONTENTS

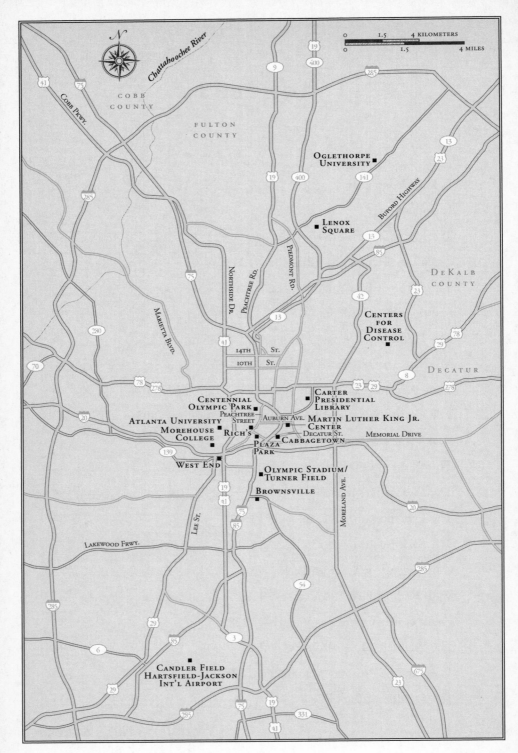

Atlanta

CONTENTS

ACKNOWLEDGMENTS

I am most grateful, as ever, to my friend and editor, Erin Turner, who was instrumental in my writing this book. I am also grateful to my editor at Globe Pequot, Meredith Rufino, who has been a gracious and kind partner in producing this work. As always, the staffs of the Kenan Research Center at the Atlanta History Center and the Georgia Department of Archives and History have been most gracious and deeply helpful with all of my queries.

Stephanie Key and Phyllis McKay were both very gracious in providing eyewitness input to some of the material in this book, and reviewing those sections for accuracy and detail. James McKay, a retired engineer formerly at WSB Radio, was a world of help in providing insight into that world, as was Peggy McKay in providing general input into Atlanta and the South during the 1950s and 1960s. John Adair and the men of SCV Camp 1642 in Cumming, Georgia, were most gracious in hosting a public discussion of some of the Civil War material contained here. My old friend and Georgia Fire Academy colleague, Steven "Woody" Woodworth, as well as Chris Wessels, David Rhodes, Matt Moseley, and Steve Campbell all provided a much appreciated abundance of detailed information about Atlanta Fire Department operations over the years.

As always, I am ultimately grateful to my friend, primary editor, absolute worst literary critic, and the greatest love of my life, my wife Bonnie. Without her constant, unwavering, complete support and encouragement in the face of serious and multifaceted challenges, all this would not have been possible.

INTRODUCTION

Atlanta is a city that is hard to define; it has changed its public face and community personalities often, sometimes even seasonally, since its founding shortly before the Civil War. Like children who are forced to grow up faster than their years would normally allow, Atlanta has had more than its share of growing pains and struggles to establish itself as a social commnity, a city of industry and business, a symbol for both the Old and New South, and a multifaceted entity to its native inhabitants. There's a saying about the weather here: "If you don't like it, wait ten minutes." Like other great, historical cities, trying to make a single, short summation of what Atlanta is can be like that. Not that it is or can be all things to all people, but because it has stood front and center in so many social, political, military, and even cultural upheavals, it has a mercurial and constantly changing character that cannot be easily summed up without leaving out many parts that create the whole. It is difficult, perhaps even impossible, to come up with a single encompassing nickname for the city.

Atlanta's original name and sometime nickname, Terminus, defined the city at its start as the muddy backwater end of a minor rail line. Its interim name of Marthasville was a not exactly subtle attempt at gaining political favor by naming the slightly larger back-water town after the governor's daughter, portending the hustling and self-promoting business center it would become. The name Gate City was a reference to Atlanta's becoming the economic and logistic capital of the Confederacy. The Phoenix is both the official symbol of the city and an acknowledgment of how Atlanta raised itself from the flames of war and rebuilt itself into a vibrant city bigger and better than it had been before the war. The name Capital of the South is a nod to the powerful industrial and commercial center Atlanta became by the late nineteenth century. The nickname City Too Busy To Hate was a somewhat accurate if sarcastic reference to Atlanta's relative lack of racial animosity during the Civil Rights movement of the 1950s and 1960s, when business and commerce were considered too important to be disrupted, while sweeping political and social changes were in fact taking place. The nickname City of Trees is a nod to just how heavily forested Atlanta is, compared to other urban centers across the nation. Hotlanta is an accurate reflection of the scorching temperatures experienced during the late spring through early fall seasons, while the appellation Big Peach, an apt name since Georgia is one of the leading peach-producing states, is a takeoff on New York City's nickname, the Big Apple.

Atlanta is home to 430,000 people within the city limits and 5 million in the surrounding metropolitan area. Reflect on the rich and varied history of the city, consider the booming commercial and economic center it has become for the entire southeastern United States, gaze on the sparkling towers and massive green spaces that abound in the still-growing metropolis, and marvel at the cultural and sports extravaganzas that it features throughout the year. Atlanta is neither a set piece on a historical stage nor a "city of the world," where international politics and global interests take precedence. It is a city where people build their homes and families, buy their groceries and shop the malls, walk their neighborhood streets and live out their lives. At the same time, it is not a tabula rasa, either, a blank slate in which its inhabitants live without the effects of what has gone on here before. The historical ground in Atlanta is deep, fertile, and utterly fascinating.

THE "PITCH-TREE"

1814

"Where is the original peach tree?" is a question often heard from tourists and travelers in Atlanta, and small wonder—there are well in excess of three dozen roads in metropolitan Atlanta that have "Peachtree" as part of their name, and the Georgia state nickname, "The Peach State," seems to suggest that there would be a myriad of candidates. The truth, as so often happens in history, is more mundane. There never were any pre-settlement "peach trees" in the area of what would become Atlanta.

There was, however, a large pine tree in the area that marked a military boundary, a major "highway," and a center of trade for the occasionally warring native inhabitants.

The earliest more or less permanent inhabitants of the area seem to have been Woodland Period Indians, who had established a village along the banks of the Chattahoochee River by around AD 200. These Hopewellian settlers were closely related to the other small (and some not so small) tribes that flourished through the first millennium, mostly noted for their later mound building, as seen in nearby Cartersville, and in their ceremonial stone ring forts scattered around north Georgia and the neighboring states. By the 1100s, these small Woodland tribes were displaced by the great Muscogee Creek nation, which eventually occupied almost all of what would become Georgia.

Several centuries later, sometime before the first larger groups of European settlers entered the scene, an Iroquois band from the Great Lakes region, known as the Yun-wiya (or "Real People"), filtered down into the southern Appalachians, settling in the Great Smoky Mountain region of North Carolina and Tennessee. By the mid-eighteenth century, though, with white settlers starting to come into the region, these "Cherokee" moved south and west, fighting with the northernmost Creeks for possession of what would become northern Georgia, including Atlanta. There is a theory, with some archeological evidence to support it, that a great battle was fought on top of Blood Mountain and down through Slaughter Gap in northeast Georgia (hence the names), sometime during the eighteenth century, and afterward the Cherokee controlled everything north of the Chattahoochee River.

Then, as now, the area that would become Atlanta was a hub of transportation and commerce, with a major north–south trail connecting native settlements in what today is Chattanooga, Tennessee, with large Cherokee towns at the Etowah and Allatoona Rivers, and further south to the major Lower Creek settlements in the area of what is today Columbus, Georgia. The Chattahoochee is a broad, slow-moving, and sometimes deceptively deep river that for centuries had a known safe crossing at what was called Shallow Ford, near present-day Roswell. This trail intersected a major east–west trail a few miles south, just west of a steep-sided hill then known as Hog Ridge (and today known as Five Points, in the middle of downtown Atlanta), a few miles west of the prominent Rock Mountain, now known as Stone Mountain. Close to this intersection, atop a bluff where Peachtree Creek joins the Chattahoochee River, and marked by an exceptionally large resin, or pitch-bearing pine tree, stood a large, sprawling Creek village known as Standing Pitch-Tree, which marked the northernmost outpost of that once-dominant nation.

Although there were thriving white settlements along the Georgia coast, and up the lower Chattahoochee to present-day Columbus, there was little interest during the colonial and Revolutionary periods in this more remote area, with no known exploitable resources, and hilly terrain and rocky soil that was hard to farm along the banks of a non-navigable river. This all changed with a renewed Indian war that merged into the second fight for American independence. Muscogee Creeks in the Ohio Valley and upper Midwest began clashing with one of their own tribes, the Red Sticks, who were attempting to break relations with the whites and return the nation to its aboriginal ways. This Creek civil war spilled over into the U.S. and British conflict on August 30, 1813, when British-supported and British-supplied Red Stick warriors attacked a U.S. installation, Fort Mims, just north of present-day Mobile, Alabama, slaughtering hundreds of mixed-race Creeks and white settlers. Since the regular U.S. Army was fully engaged in the War of 1812 by then, frontier militias from Georgia, Mississippi Territory, and Tennessee were called out, supplemented by Cherokees, Lower Creeks, and Choctaw Indians, all under the command of General Andrew Jackson.

Georgia started its military response by establishing a series of forts along its frontier line on the Chattahoochee River, from Columbus north to near present-day Dacula. In 1814, a tiny force of twenty-two soldiers from the 43rd Infantry under Lieutenant George R. Gilmer (later a two-term governor of Georgia), built a small, quite crude log fort in the area of Standing Pitch-Tree, inside what is today the Atlanta Water Works. It was originally named Fort Gilmer, after the young commander, but he renamed it Fort Peachtree, possibly the first recorded instance of the name confusion. It was unimpressive even for a low-threat frontier site. Sergeant James McConnell Montgomery of Gilmer's small command later wrote a report to General Jackson, stating that the outpost had a good tactical siting and a "romantic" view of the river for a commanding distance. In the same report, he described the post as: "two large hew'd logg block houses, six dwelling houses, one fram'd store house, one bridge . . . and five boats" that cost the government "not less than five thousand dollars."

It was small wonder that the outpost was not architecturally impressive. Gilmer was later quoted as saying that he "had never seen a fort" before building his own! The cost was a bargain for the Georgia government, about $50,500 in today's currency, an amount which underscored the perceived unimportance and lack of sophistication of the very remote fortification. Postwar deployment and installation drawdowns are not a new concept; this small outpost was abandoned the following year without ever seeing action, even before all the fighting in this second struggle against the British was completed. It was resurrected briefly fifty years later, this time as a Confederate fortification during the Battle of Peachtree Creek. Sergeant Montgomery came back into the area after his military service, appointed as postmaster for the fledgling town of Standing Peachtree; he also ran a side business transporting travelers across the river, at Montgomery's Ferry.

Peach trees are native to China, introduced to parts of Europe by Alexander the Great, and then finally brought to America in the seventeenth century, where they were first planted in Virginia. They were first commercially grown in Georgia nearly a hundred years later, long after the "Pitch-Tree" had already been misunderstood, and the name indelibly attached to the area.

TERMINUS BECOMES MARTHASVILLE

1843

It didn't really start with Benjamin Parks's hunting trip.

North Georgia had been ceded to the Cherokee Nation since a pair of treaties were signed in 1777 (Treaties of DeWitt's Corner and Long Island), in part because no white settler thought the rocky, mountainous area was good for very much. Although the vast lands occupied by the Cherokee had been whittled down through the years by a nearly endless series of treaties (and subsequently, broken treaties), most of the lands lying to the north and west of the Chattahoochee River, including what would become the northern metro Atlanta area, were thought to be relatively safe from the ever-encroaching white settlements.

The Lower Creek Nation, on the other hand, weakened by infighting and distrust of whites, and constantly threatened by their ancient foes in the Cherokee Nation, finally gave up. The Treaty of Indian Spring was signed on January 18, 1821, giving up all Creek claims in Georgia, which included everything south and east of the

Chattahoochee River. Although most of this land was hardscrabble frontier so far as the whites were concerned, it didn't take long for some to stake their claims as far north as possible. Just four years later, Standing Peachtree became an official town, when J.M.C. Montgomery opened a U.S. Post Office next to his ferry business already established there.

Although the land north of the Chattahoochee was theoretically off limits to whites, there were a number of missionaries, whites friendly to the Cherokee, and even a handful of isolated white farms in the area. One of these whites that traveled in the territory was Benjamin Parks, who had permission to hunt on Cherokee land. One day in December 1828, walking over a hill just west of the Chestatee River near modern day Dahlonega, Parks stumbled across an unusual, very shiny rock lying on the ground. It was gold, highly pure gold at that, and his announcement of the discovery kicked off the first major gold rush in America, twenty years before the more famous California rush.

There had been a smaller gold rush in North Carolina after deposits were found there in 1799, but the Georgia rush was kicked into high gear by the fact that so much ore was what was known as "placer," deposits found easily in rivers and streams or simply lying open on the ground. By 1830, there were well over four thousand miners in the Dahlonega area alone, with many thousands more staking claims along the Chestatee, Etowah, and Chattahoochee Rivers as far south as Fulton County. Within a few years, this number would more than triple, with contiguous deposits found as far west as eastern Alabama. The major problem was that almost all of this land belonged to the Cherokee Nation.

At first the Cherokee Nation tried to keep the swarming hordes of miners out of their territory with very limited help (and, in short order, opposition) from the state government, but the issue was finally settled when its land was simply stripped from it. The federal government had made a deal with Georgia in 1802, promising to remove all the native inhabitants from the state in exchange for Georgia's dropping claims to its western lands, which became Alabama and Mississippi. Despite this, there was little popular sentiment to claim all the northern mountainous land until this discovery of gold. After the state ordered all the Cherokee out, the Nation sued in federal court, culminating in an Indian victory in the *Worchester v. Georgia* case. Chief Justice John Marshall stated in his majority opinion that the Indians had sovereignty over the territory, and that they could not simply be removed. President Andrew Jackson, a fierce political enemy of Marshall, ignored the ruling, and was alleged to say about it, "John Marshall has made his decision; now let him (or 'his armies') enforce it!" Georgia held a land lottery that same year for all this "new" property and ordered the state militia to round up all the remaining Indians in the state.

Despite the worrisome prospect of Indian raids and uprisings in this frontier territory, settlements and small towns popped up all through the late 1820s and early 1830s. Standing Peachtree was already established as a small business and ferry crossing, but Atlanta really drew its roots from Hardy Ivey, who built his first cabin in 1833 a few miles east, atop Hog Ridge, at what today is the corner of Courtland Avenue and International Boulevard in the heart of downtown. The gold strikes had started the opening of all of northern Georgia to white settlement, but what really drove the buildup was the massive increase in trade and commerce surrounding the gold-mining industry. Two years after Ivey settled, Charner Humphries built a tavern to serve the increasing numbers of travelers in the area; this small building at the corner of modern-day Gordon and Lee Streets was named a post office in June of 1835.

The Georgia Legislature, responding to the rapid growth of business in these newly opened areas, in 1836 approved financing to build a railroad to connect Tennessee with the Chattahoochee River at Standing Peachtree. The original thought was that this "State Road" would connect to the river, which would be opened to commercial traffic from Columbus. Before a single mile of rail was laid, however, careful surveys proved that this would be a futile effort. Instead, a second proposal was quickly adopted by the legislature, establishing a second "road" from Augusta through Eatonton to connect to the northern road, and a third line north from Macon and Savannah that would further connect the great cities in the east with the quickly growing frontier territories.

Colonel Stephen Harriman Long was given the task of surveying the route in May 1837, and work began on the line by July, even before the entire route had been determined. At first, Long intended to place the "terminus" of the line in the area of Hog Mountain, near present day Norcross, but even as work began, it became apparent that the hilly terrain and multiple creeks and rivers would make it simply too expensive to build there. Instead, Long determined the most economically feasible site would be just east of Montgomery's Ferry and received permission from Hardy Ivey to relocate the end of the line to his farm. Long's assistant, Albert Brisbane, drove the "Zero Mile" stake in Ivey's donated property on September 19, 1837. The town of Terminus was established in that simple act.

The growth of both the town and rail line was slow through the rest of the 1830s, as railroad construction was held up by both technical difficulties and political infighting in the legislature. Various politicians wanted the terminal point of the railroad moved south to Henry County, all the way to Macon, or southeast to the state capital at Milledgeville. A former Georgia governor, Wilson Lumpkin, took over operation of the railroad in 1842, replaced the officers and chief engineer, and kicked off real progress in construction. His new chief engineer, Fenton Mercer Garnett, set up his office at the Whitehall Tavern in Terminus and proposed renaming the settlement something more conducive to attracting settlers and business— Marthasville. It was not a coincidence that Lumpkin's strikingly beautiful teenage daughter was named Martha! This was accepted and approved by the state legislature in 1845, with the first elections in the now rapidly growing town taking place in 1847. Lumpkin accepted another land donation, this time from Samuel Mitchell, as the final location of the railroad terminus, at the modern-day corner of Pryor Street and Central Avenue, where the old Union Station was later built. Ironically, the growth of Marthasville began just as the gold rush in Georgia was starting to die down. The "gold rush" of mineral wealth was soon supplemented and replaced by the rush for commercial wealth.

For all the celebration of Parks's discovery, the truth is that north Georgia gold fields were known well before his late 1828 hunting trip. There are no records of who made the first "discovery" (other than the Cherokee, of course), but a quiet, and illegal, mining operation was already underway by 1819 near the Cherokee village of Sixes, near modern-day Canton. The opening of the gold fields to widespread exploitation did lead to the opening of central and northern Georgia to settlement, areas that had been previously thought to be barren and undesirable, and very directly to the establishment of Atlanta as a city. Parks's claim to fame was primarily the result of his ceaseless marketing of himself as making the first discovery, for the last seventy years of his life. In that, he was very much in the mold of modern Atlanta business!

THE BATTLE OF EAST ATLANTA

1864

By the late spring of 1864, even after the nearly simultaneous Union victories at Gettysburg and Vicksburg the year before, the war was not going well for the North. Confederate General Robert E. Lee had successfully avoided being pinned down and annihilated, ever since his army had retreated out of Pennsylvania, and in the west, Confederate armies in Tennessee, Georgia, and Mississippi had fought their Union counterparts to a near standstill. The only thing that seemed to be significantly higher for the Union armies were the casualty lists, and President Abraham Lincoln was increasingly being blamed for dragging the Union into an unwinnable morass of endless warfare, without having any sort of "exit strategy." To top everything off, 1864 was an election year in the North, and Lincoln's chief rival, Union Major General George B. McClellan, an immensely popular war hero, was running as a "War Democrat," who promised to sue for peace and end the fighting as soon as he could take office. Something spectacular would have to happen that summer, or the war would end in a Confederate victory.

While fighting raged across the nation and into the far western territories, the main bulk of combat was concentrated in two areas: to the east and southeast of the Confederate capital at Richmond, and in the far northwest of Georgia, near Chattanooga. Following his decisive victories at Vicksburg and Chattanooga, Lincoln entrusted his entire Union army to a single commander, newly promoted Lieutenant General Ulysses S. Grant. Grant immediately laid out a comprehensive plan to defeat the Confederate armies, and to do so quickly, before the election, and the Union itself, was lost. The two main Confederate armies, Lee's Army of Northern Virginia and General Joseph E. Johnston's Army of Tennessee, would be directly targeted by the bulk of his available forces, while other commands would attack Confederate lines of supply and infrastructure to further choke off their ability to fight. Grant took direct command of the armies in Virginia, while he placed his close friend, Major General William T. Sherman, in charge of the armies in the west, with orders to overwhelm the Confederate forces in the field. Sherman, a very modern general, knew that the key to this new style of warfare was supply and logistics, and that the city of Atlanta was the center of such for the Southern armies.

By late April, Grant was in full pursuit of Lee in eastern Virginia, heading toward a long-term stalemate at Petersburg. Sherman had built up an enormous force at Chattanooga, ninety-eight thousand strong organized into three grand armies, with another fourteen thousand heading to reinforce him. He planned to strike south toward Atlanta as soon as all his forces were equipped, supplied, and arrayed in place, with the aim of sticking close to the Western & Atlantic Railroad track line to better supply his huge force. That single track, extended by other single lines to his base of supply at Louisville, Kentucky, would do the work otherwise requiring nearly thirty-seven thousand wagons. He intended to use his massive force as a battering ram, to sweep aside and occupy Atlanta in as short a period as possible, and then pause to consider where next to deploy his forces.

One Confederate command stood to oppose Sherman, Johnston's battle-hardened and well-respected Army of Tennessee, fifty thousand strong, with another full corps of fifteen thousand men en route from Mississippi to reinforce him. He had a single overriding task, to protect and defend Atlanta at all costs and keep it from falling into Union hands until at least the November elections. Johnston had a great love for his army, which was well reciprocated by his men, and was a master at defensive warfare. He planned to take on Sherman with what is known as a "rolling defense." He would gradually give way under pressure, inflicting as heavy a price for each foot of land as possible, and keep his own forces intact with as few unnecessary casualties as possible. Eventually he would pull back inside the defenses of Atlanta itself, which were well under way that spring to making the city the most heavily fortified in the world. Once there, he planned to let Sherman batter his own army to pieces in futile assaults, bleeding itself dry and filling the Northern newspapers with long lists of the dead, wounded, and missing, until the Confederacy was ultimately spared through Union political weaknesses.

The Campaign for Atlanta kicked off on May 8, Sherman's forces moving south from their deployments between Tunnel Hill and Ringgold, heading toward the small town of Dalton. Sherman soon showed his preferred tactic, which was to hold the Confederate forces in place with part of his force while simultaneously launching an attack on their side flank or rear with other forces, with the intent to drive Johnston away from the railroad tracks and crush him whenever possible. Johnston also showed his own preferred tactic, which was to hold a position long enough for Sherman to deploy for a major blow, inflict as many Union casualties as possible, and then quickly withdraw south before Sherman's forces could entrap and destroy him.

Through the month of May, the two armies fought at Resaca, Cassville, the Etowah River crossing, Kingston, Rome, and Allatoona Pass, before arriving in Acworth, northwest of Marietta. There Sherman paused briefly, knowing the terrain intimately (he had been a young Army engineering officer assigned to Marietta long before the war); he realized that nearby Kennesaw Mountain was a formidable barrier to his progress, not easily bypassed and even less easily taken. In late May, he ordered his armies westward, hoping to sneak past Johnston's lines of defense and cut him off from Atlanta. Johnston, soon learning of the Union redeployment, moved his own forces westward, met and decisively defeated Sherman's forces at New Hope Church and Pickett's Mill, near Dallas. Sherman retreated to his rail line of supply, and tried once again, this time assaulting the flanks of Kennesaw Mountain itself, only to be pushed back again in late June with heavy casualties.

Frustrated, Sherman returned to his "hold 'em and flank 'em" tactics, this time successfully bypassing Kennesaw Mountain to the west, and causing Johnston to have to hurry and get south of the Chattahoochee River before Sherman could cut him off there. In three weeks of near continuous combat, Sherman pushed his Confederate foes south of Marietta and the river, and keeping the pressure on, even further south, nearly to the gates of Atlanta itself, before Johnston was able to reestablish his lines once again to make a strong stand. It was here, at Peachtree Creek on July 17, just as he was preparing to launch an unusual offensive move against a weakness his cavalry scouts had found in Sherman's lines, that Johnston's other problem arose.

Confederate President Jefferson Davis was a bitter political enemy of Johnston, but the reasons are not clear exactly why. One of

Johnston's subordinates, Major General John Bell Hood, was an old, trusted, and close friend of Davis, and had been sending him nearly constant letters of complaint about Johnston's strategies. Hood, well known as a "fighting general," chafed under the disciplined defensive tactics, wanting to take the fight out to the far superior Union forces, a tactic that pretty much everyone else, including his own men, knew would be a disaster. Davis, also irritated at Johnston's tactics, and fearing Atlanta and thus the Confederacy would be lost if they continued, fired Johnston on July 17, replacing him with Hood. Hood took three more days to redeploy his army, losing the slight tactical advantage against Sherman that Johnston had spotted, and launching an all-out attack against the Union forces on July 20. It was a disaster. Thick woods and underbrush made it impossible for the Confederate unit commanders to coordinate their attacks properly, and the Union troops had deeply entrenched, in case of such an assault. Johnston had suffered relatively few casualties all along the fighting retreat, nearly 100 miles south from Dalton, but Hood managed to lose 4,800 men in this single, ill-conceived battle. Before the battle was even concluded, Sherman once again sent part of his force sweeping around the eastern flank of the city, engaging Confederate cavalry on a small hilltop between Atlanta and Decatur, and deployed his heavy artillery to start bombarding the center of the city itself.

The following day, with Sherman's forces threatening once again to get between him and the city, Hood pulled his troops south inside the defenses of Atlanta, abandoning the Western & Atlantic Railroad line to Sherman. Then as night fell, he marched through the city southwards, turning east on the DeKalb Road, panicking the town residents who feared he was abandoning them to the dread Union army. Hood had no intention of leaving; he was planning another frontal assault to destroy or drive away Sherman's vastly superior force, this time as they were settling into a line of battle crossing the road to Decatur. On July 22, he launched his attack, the "Battle of Atlanta," or more accurately, the Battle of East Atlanta.

Sherman already had a powerful line of entrenchments dug along what is today Moreland Avenue, with his own headquarters in the Augustus Hurt House on the grounds of what is today the Carter Presidential Library. Given Hood's fiery reputation, the Union commanders were concerned that he would indeed launch an attack in this area, even as their main attention was focused on getting ready to set up heavy siege cannons and redeploying their troops to prepare for all-out assaults on any weak point that could be found in the Atlanta defenses. Sherman's close friend, Major General James Birdseye McPherson, deployed his Army of the Tennessee across DeKalb Avenue, in the vicinity of what is today Little Five Points, awaiting Hood's assault.

Hood had planned to attack at dawn, but due to confusion on the unmarked roads, exhaustion among his men, and the killing of a critical division commander by a Union sniper just as dawn broke, the attack did not commence until 12:15 p.m. The attack here was no more successful than the one two days before at Peachtree Creek. With few exceptions, the Union lines held firm, and Confederate forces were thrown back with heavy losses before the afternoon was out. Sherman's major loss was that of McPherson himself, killed in action when he and his staff accidentally blundered into the path of one of the Confederate breakthroughs. As the day ended, Hood pulled back into the city defenses, leaving more than five thousand casualties behind, and losing one more critical rail line, the Georgia Railroad connecting Augusta with the city. Atlanta, the wartime center of transportation and supply, was down to its last two open rail lines, the Macon & Western to the south, and the Atlanta & West Point connecting to the southwest.

Over the next month, Hood tried to defend his last two remaining rail supply lines into the city against Sherman's tightening cordon. Sherman knew he could not hope to batter his way into the city, which by then had three strong belts of trench lines, artillery emplacements, and fortresses surrounding it. The Union forces attempted successfully to draw Hood out to fight, and combat erupted at Ezra Church on July 28, Utoy Creek on August 6, and, finally, at Jonesboro on August 31. Each day since July 20, heavy Union guns had thrown tons of explosive ordnance inside the city, creating overwhelming stress and misery, and killing untold numbers of civilians.

Atlanta, over that long sweltering summer, would become the most heavily bombarded city ever in the Western Hemisphere.

SHERMAN BURNS ATLANTA

1864

Early on the morning of Friday, September 2, 1864, Atlanta Mayor James M. Calhoun and a handful of city leaders rode slowly down the now-quiet, shell-blasted Marietta Street, carrying a white flag of surrender. Jonesboro had fallen to Federal troops two days previously, and with it the last rail line out of Atlanta was gone, followed in short order by Lieutenant General John Bell Hood and the surviving ranks of his Confederate Army of Tennessee. Calhoun and his small band of riders passed through the now-deserted earthworks and redoubts guarding the main avenue, and then found who they were looking for near the corner of what is today Marietta and Howell Mill Road, a troop of Federal cavalry scouts.

Since July 20, the city had been subjected to nearly continuous heavy shell fire, sometimes as many as five thousand rounds a day slamming into the heart of the town. The very first round was fired from the Illinois Artillery Battery commanded by Captain Francis DeGress; he would probably have been aggrieved to know that this initial shell burst killed a little girl walking with her parents at the corner of East Ellis and Ivy Streets. Casualties over the following thirty-six days of siege had been surprisingly low, only about twenty civilians killed and perhaps five hundred or so wounded to one degree or another, but few buildings on any given block were completely spared from at least some damage.

Four great battles had raged around the city during that five-week period, in East Atlanta, Ezra Church and Utoy Creek to the west, and finally at Jonesboro on the south side, but the well-constructed works encircling the city held firm, allowing no Union troops within a mile of the center of town. The summer before, with the war turning out badly for the Confederacy, an engineering officer, Captain Lemuel P. Grant, was ordered to the city to make plans for its defense in case of an expected invasion. Although a native of Maine, Grant had been an engineer with two Georgia railroads since 1840 and had become a decidedly devout Southern partisan. Grant quickly planned and began construction of a great ring of fortifications around Atlanta, two and three layers thick in places, with nearly continuous lines of infantry entrenchment, artillery emplacements, and well-reinforced redoubts, all secured behind cleared lanes of fire and rows of abatis, closely arranged rows of sharpened stakes, and "chevaux-de-frise," an early, wooden version of concertina wire. Using thousands of Confederate engineers and slaves rented from their owners for twenty-five dollars per month, about seven miles of defensive works were in place by November, when Grant reported to his superiors:

> *The Defenses of Atlanta consist of Redoubts and Rifle*
> *Pits. The former (are) generally intended for five guns*
> *each. The contour of the eminences around the City*
> *is such that the redoubts seemed to me to be the most*
> *economical plan. Of these, we have 17, of which 4 are*

unfinished. The length of the line is about 7½ miles,
averaging about 1½ miles from the center of the city.

By April 1864, Grant was able to report that his extensive planned works were nearing completion, but this work was interrupted by Sherman's invasion the next month. The fiery Ohioan had planned to assault the city when he arrived at the gates in late July, but this hope was dashed by a detailed report of the city's defenses from his own chief of engineering, Captain Orlando M. Poe, which left him with no hope of blasting his way in. Poe wrote in his postwar memoirs:

> *(The Confederate works) completely encircled the city*
> *at a distance of about one and a half miles from the*
> *center and consisted of a system of batteries, open to the*
> *rear and connected by infantry parapets, with complete*
> *abatis, in some places in three or four rows, with rows*
> *of pointed stakes, and long lines of chevaux-de-frise.*
> *In many places rows of palisading were planted along*
> *the foot of the exterior slope of the infantry parapet*
> *with sufficient openings between the timbers to permit*
> *the infantry fire, if carefully delivered, to pass freely*
> *through it, but not sufficient to permit a person to pass*
> *through, and having a height of twelve to fourteen feet.*
> *The ground in front of these palisades was always com-*
> *pletely swept by fire from the adjacent batteries, which*
> *enabled a very small force to hold them.*

Instead, Sherman turned to cutting off Atlanta from resupply and reinforcement by taking the four rail lines leading into the city, and setting up heavy siege guns to blast the city to rubble until it surrendered. He did not have the luxury of time, though, that he and Grant had enjoyed at Vicksburg the year before, as the specter of a presidential election and a potential political end to the war that gave the victory to the Confederacy hung over his head. Rather than setting up his own fixed line of entrenchments, he kept his army maneuvering around the city for the next month, daring Hood to come out and fight, which the rash and headstrong Confederate commander was all too willing to do. While Hood should have stuck to the plan, staying inside his entrenchments, enduring the pounding artillery fire, and waiting for the November election, he instead wasted his precious manpower in dribs and drabs, sending out inadequate forces to counter Sherman's moves, wasting an army in such futile measures. Hood had been badly injured at Gettysburg in July 1863, losing the use of his left arm; just two months later he lost most of his left leg at Chickamauga. Due to his extensive injuries, he had become hooked on the painkiller laudanum. A very bold, aggressive field commander before his injuries, he was now under great pressure to stay defensive and not to surrender the city under any circumstance. Not a few of his own men whispered that he had "gone mad" from the combination of drugs and stress.

Hood fell completely into Sherman's trap. With the fall of Jonesboro on August 31, and one full corps (of three) of his army cut off outside the city in a foolish bid to keep the rail line there open, Hood no longer had the manpower left to adequately man the defenses. On September 1, he gave the order to withdraw south to McDonough, then on to Lovejoy, where the troops would redeploy to meet an expected further attack by Sherman. The remnant of his army moved out that afternoon and evening, spiking the heavy guns they were now unable to take with them. As the rear guard left the southeastern defensive works, his engineers blew up the last trainloads of military supplies left inside the city. Five locomotives and eighty-one boxcars full of shot and powder exploded in a din heard by Sherman himself miles away in Jonesboro, and lit up the sky with fires that burned through the night. Every building around the Georgia Railroad depot, near what is today Oakland Cemetery, was either leveled or heavily damaged by the blasts, and several whole blocks of the city around the depot burned to the ground in the aftermath.

The next morning Mayor Calhoun left on his mission to formally surrender the city to prevent any further destruction as the Union armies entered. He surrendered to Captain Henry M. Scott, the inspector general of Brigadier General William T. Ward's 3rd Division (XX Corps), and with very little armed opposition, columns of Union troops were soon pouring into the city. Sherman was informed that the city was under federal occupation on September 3 and issued an order formally ending the Atlanta Campaign. He quickly set about remaking Atlanta into a military city, expelling civilians and bringing in supplies by the ton-load from his base at Nashville, over the newly repaired and heavily guarded Western & Atlantic Railroad line. As summer turned into fall, Hood took the remnants of his battered army northward, futilely hoping to draw Sherman out of the city. Sherman sent out one corps to chase his defeated foe farther away, cackling with delight as Hood moved farther and farther away from the occupied city, "If he will go to the Ohio River, I will give him rations!"

Despite this gloating, Sherman did have a problem: where to go next. He couldn't afford to stay in Atlanta much longer with an undefeated Army of Tennessee under Hood still lurking about, reduced as it may have been. He was also under heavy political pressure to move south across the state and relieve the Union prisoners at the notorious prison camp at Andersonville, but was reluctant to do so. He lacked resources to handle his own army in that part of the state and had no easy place to transport the prisoners afterward.

He finally settled on a fast-moving campaign, sweeping south by east across the middle portion of Georgia toward Savannah, stripping the countryside of resources to feed his army as they moved. He reduced his own force to a comparatively lean sixty thousand, and sent the rest up to Nashville under Major General George H. "Pap" Thomas, where they would face and defeat Hood's army in December.

As they prepared to leave on the "March to the Sea" toward Savannah, Sherman gave Poe an order to destroy anything left of military value in the city. Poe took the order very liberally, wantonly destroying most of the remaining structures, starting the afternoon of November 11 without any objection from his higher command. One gets the idea that Sherman winked as he gave the "military value" order. To complete the destruction more thoroughly and efficiently, Poe quickly developed a new machine consisting of a twenty-one-foot-long iron bar, swinging on chains from a ten-foot-high wooden scaffold. With gangs of soldiers to move and swing the device, it was a clever way to knock down and reduce to unusable rubble any building they selected. The railroad roundhouse, factories, ware-houses, residences, and masonry buildings of all description were soon reduced to piles of rubble. In these and other buildings, Union soldiers piled stacks of mattresses, oil-soaked wagon parts, broken fence rails, and just about anything else that would burn.

Finally ready to move out on November 15, Sherman ordered Poe to start burning the city late that afternoon. Within a few minutes, these "authorized" fires had been set, at first confined to factories and warehouses in the central business district around Whitehall Street. An early evening wind soon built up the fires, spraying sparks and burning cinders in every direction. Visibly pleased by the sight of the out-of-control fires raging through the city, Sherman was moved to remark only that he supposed the flames would be visible from Griffin, about forty-five miles to the south.

As the huge fire built, block after block exploded into flame. What initially escaped the "authorized" fires, did not escape the wind-whipped cinders and some "unauthorized" fires started by freelancing soldiers, who burned homes and businesses to cover up their also "unauthorized" ransacking and looting. In the midst of the smoke, flame, terrified horses, and shouting men, the 33rd Massachusetts Regimental Band stood calmly and righteously playing "John Brown's Soul Goes Marching On." Major George Ward Nichols, Sherman's aide-de-camp, remarked without a hint of sarcasm that he had "never heard that noble anthem when it was so grand, so solemn, so inspiring."

As the flames died down overnight, dawn revealed that over 4,100 of the 4,500 buildings in town had been leveled by the flames, including every single business. Sherman mounted his horse, Sam, and with a last look at the July 22 battlefield east of the city, where his close friend James McPherson had died, led his men out of the ruins, bound for Savannah and the Atlantic Ocean.

THE FOUNDING OF ATLANTA UNIVERSITY

1865

With the fall and surrender of the Confederacy in April 1865, the military struggle ended but the longer and harder struggle to rebuild the almost completely destroyed South began. Atlanta had already begun replacing critical infrastructure destroyed the year before, a task complicated by a severe shortage of money and supplies. When Mayor James Calhoun was elected for his fourth term in December, there was only $1.64 in the city's treasury. The economic situation was compounded by Union troops occupying the city, who were not primarily interested in helping rebuild quickly; thousands of wounded and paroled Confederate soldiers passing through every week, some with nowhere else to go; and even more newly freed ex-slaves, who drifted into the city from the countryside, looking for new homes and livelihoods.

To add to the misery, the first Union military commander over Georgia was Major General James H. Wilson, a famed cavalry commander and one of the few to ever best Confederate cavalryman

Nathan Bedford Forrest. Wilson was by far the most widely despised man in Georgia, eclipsing Sherman and disliked even by the small population of nominal Union supporters in Atlanta, due primarily to his actions during Wilson's Raid. This large cavalry action swept across Alabama and Georgia in the spring of 1865, assaulting and taking five fortified towns; destroying 115,000 bales of cotton, eight major factories, and a massive amount of railroad stock and equipment; reducing the University of Alabama to a smoldering ruin; and capturing nearly seven thousand prisoners in a seemingly wanton orgy of nearly unopposed violence, most of which took place after Confederate General Robert E. Lee had surrendered his army in Virginia. Cavalrymen under Wilson's command eventually captured Confederate President Jefferson Davis near Irwinville, Georgia, several weeks later, ensuring that there would be not a peep of protest from Northern politicians over Wilson's destructive inclinations.

Lost in the postwar turmoil at first was the situation of thousands of newly freed slaves. Sherman had begun a process of slave liberation and economic recovery during his fall 1864 Georgia Campaign; while on the march to Savannah, he "liberated" hundreds from plantations subsequently destroyed along the way and "allowed" them to serve as laborers for his own forces, mostly involuntarily. In January 1865, when Savannah and most of the coastline of Georgia was secured, Sherman issued an order that selected plots of land and certain farm properties running south from Charleston to Jacksonville, Florida, were to be divided up among their former enslaved inhabitants, thus giving each former slave "forty acres and a mule." Despite the liberal sound of this written order, it was never intended to be a general policy (and was never codified into law by Congress). It was meant exclusively to settle the turmoil caused by military campaigning in these areas, and not coincidentally, free Sherman from the burden of caring for the thousands of freed slaves, known as "contraband," that were flocking to his armies.

Lincoln's assassination and the subsequent political uproar in April 1865 squashed any hope of a fair and equitable end to the war for any Southerner, white or black, "seceesh" or Union supporter.

The new president, Andrew Johnson, although a Southerner from Tennessee, quickly ordered an end to the "forty acres and a mule" programs Sherman and others had begun. Johnson was the only Southerner to remain loyal to the Union and in Congress after the secession of the Confederacy, and thus was distrusted by most Northerners and utterly loathed by most Southerners. His initial plans to reunite the country were seen as far too soft on the South by his Radical Republican opponents in Congress and were soon overturned in favor of "making the South howl," in the words of Sherman himself. Harsh demands for policies that would render the South politically impotent and helpless were soon imposed by the reactionary Congress, with little to no consideration given to how these policies would affect the nation as a whole. One of the few nonpunitive measures implemented in the South was the Freedmen's Bureau Bill, originally passed by Congress and signed by Abraham Lincoln five weeks before he was assassinated. It set up the "Bureau of Refugees, Freedmen, and Abandoned Lands," more familiarly known as the Freedmen's Bureau, a military-run social services agency designed to bring the freed slaves quickly into some form of parity in the rebuilding of the Southern economy. It was supposed to help with obtaining adequate housing, health care, food, and education, and to serve as a legal court in settling contractual disputes between white landowners and black workers.

Just because the agency was meant to be nonpunitive did not mean that it was always seen or used that way or was entirely successful. Although it made practical sense for the military to run this social service organization (something similar to the "nation building" efforts we see today, except using combat troops instead of specially trained civil affairs specialists), the Army was in the midst of fighting a newly hot Indian War in both the Southwest and the Plains and in no mood to leave its best officers behind to run the Freedmen's Bureau. General Oliver Otis "Uh-Oh" Howard was given command of the new bureau; he was an honorable man who displayed a great Christian piety, but had been a poor battlefield leader. His sub-commanders were by and large drawn from the ranks of those not seen as fit for the intense fighting in the West, and who played a large part in creating the subsequent record of the Bureau, one riddled with graft, corruption, dereliction of duty, and overall failure.

One of the few areas in which the Bureau did have some success was in education. Before the war, no Southern state had any systematic form of public education, and most had laws banning the education of slaves. These newly liberated men and women had a burning desire to become literate, despite the vocal opposition of the former white elites of the South. To fill this need, abolitionist organizations flooded the South with idealistic teachers and Christian missionaries. One of the most effective of these organizations was the American Missionary Association (AMA), which sent Massachusetts Reverend Frederick Ayer to Atlanta for the express purpose of building public "colored" schools. He was soon joined by Reverend Erasmus M. Cravath and two young female teachers, Rose and Lucy Kinney of Ohio. Ayer bought an old boxcar for the princely sum of $310 ($4,294.42 in 2009 dollars!), where he set up his first classrooms in November 1865, next to the newly formed Friendship Baptist Church between Cain and Luckie Streets. The two new institutions shared both physical space and a close kinship; these crude beginnings were the first "Negro schools" that had existed in Georgia and were the fertile ground on which further institutions of higher learning would be founded. Ayer, however, was an older man by the time he started his work in Atlanta, and the AMA soon had to send a replacement, Edmund Asa Ware.

Howard's Freedmen's Bureau had at first been poorly funded by Congress, but his allied Radical Republicans, reacting to President Johnson's nearly total opposition, provided adequate funds by 1867. Ware had already begun discussions about building the first "Negro" college and was convinced in April of that year to take on a role with the Freedmen's Bureau to help bring this about. Howard was in danger of being sacked, however, and Johnson sought to defund the entire program, so time was running short. Howard appointed Ware as the "Superintendent of Schools for the Freedmen's Bureau in Georgia," which not only gave him access to funds from the AMA but also further directed government funds, and a prestigious position in which to lobby for further educational funding. Almost single-handedly, he promoted the idea of a formally recognized college to further the abilities of black scholars in three specific areas: "(1) train talented Negro youth, (2) educate teachers, and (3) disseminate civilization among the untaught masses." To this purpose, Ware and ten other men petitioned the Fulton County Superior Court for a charter of incorporation as the "Trustees of the Atlanta University." It was granted without opposition on October 16, 1867.

Atlanta University began in the ashes of the destroyed city in its first incarnation as a basic school for teaching literacy and essential civic duties. Within four years, it grew into the first primarily black institution granting graduate degrees in the United States, with the committed backing of religious organizations and the government of the United States. In doing so, it became one of the only highlights in the history of the idealistic intentions of the Freedmen's Bureau, which was abolished in 1872.

MORRIS RICH OPENS
HIS GENERAL STORE

1867

By 1867 Atlanta's rebuilding efforts following the Civil War were well underway. Whitehall Street, the former main business district, had been reduced to a smoldering ruin with only a single intact block remaining by the time Sherman's forces departed, but had started a rapid rebuilding almost as soon as Johnston's armies finally surrendered a half year later. A German-Jewish immigrant from Hungary, Morris Rich, arrived in the rebuilding city after wandering through Tennessee and Georgia peddling various small goods. Something about Atlanta appealed to Rich enough to inspire him to put down some roots there.

Barely three years after the Battle of Atlanta and its subsequent nearly complete destruction by fire, there was a rapidly growing commercial business boom going on, primarily due to the influx of Northern "Carpetbaggers" and the Southern "scalawags" who did business with them. The city was able to report that nearly 250 businesses had reopened or established themselves since the end of the war, helping to reverse the severe economic depression that had gripped Atlanta since the middle of the war years. Rich chose a vacant lot on Whitehall Street, the avenue that had been the prewar central business district, to build his first store. Lacking the funds and the time to build a more substantial structure, he borrowed $500 from his brother William and set up a hasty, rough-sawed, pine-framed, twenty-by-seventy-five foot building, directly next to what today would be Plaza Park. Rich remarked later that for days before he opened his store, it had been raining torrentially, and he risked some of his small remaining capital to lay down a board sidewalk over the thick, red clay mud on the side of the street, so his potential customers might find an easier path to his door.

On May 28, 1867, M. Rich Dry Goods opened its doors for the first time, and despite the postwar economic problems, customers did indeed find a way to his door. At first, his best-selling goods were inexpensive corsets and hosiery, for the proper but broke ladies of the rebuilding city. The brief wartime boomtown emphasis on luxury goods had given way to far more mundane concerns over iron pots and washboards, which Rich soon stocked in affordable abundance. His small store had serious competition from larger and much better stocked establishments popping up all along Whitehall Street, but Rich was one of the few that extended "market credit" for anything in his store, an old farming tradition where bills would be settled once a year after the crops had come in. Rich was soon able to hire his first employee, his cousin Adolph Teitlebaum, but lived with William for a number of years, pouring his profits into the business. Four years later, his younger brother Emanuel joined the growing business, followed by a third brother, Daniel, in 1876, prompting the renaming of the store to M. Rich & Brothers Company.

The Rich brothers soon outgrew the first crude building, after continually adding on and expanding; they moved to what became their flagship store on Peachtree Street in 1881. One *Atlanta Constitution* reporter tagged it as the "handsomest store in Atlanta." The first business in Atlanta to have large plate glass windows along its frontage on Peachtree, it inspired the first "window shoppers" by displaying goods and fashions in these dedicated window displays. In 1924 with business still increasing steadily, the Rich brothers moved to their final main location, a six-story, $1.5-million edifice located at Broad and Alabama Streets, and connected to annexes along adjoining Whitehall and Hunter Streets.

Cash being scarce, Rich also cheerfully accepted produce and farm products as barter, establishing a tradition that would eventually endear him and his business to legions of Atlanta residents. In 1967, an *Atlanta Constitution* columnist and Atlanta icon, Celestine Sibley, published a book about the history of Rich's the title of which summed up how nearly everyone felt about the business, *Dear Store: An Affectionate Portrait of Rich's*. In it, she outlined how Morris continued his liberal policies in the face of later economic disasters. Following a cotton market crash in 1914, Rich's announced that it would take farmer's unsellable cotton in kind the same as cash. Morris's nephew Walter took over the business in 1926 and immediately set about expanding Morris's civic awareness and community trust even further. During the Great Depression of the 1930s, Atlanta found itself unable to pay its schoolteachers. Walter called the mayor, told him to pay the teachers in script, which he would then exchange for cash with no strings attached to spend it in his store. He also loaned the city $654,000 so the teacher payroll could be met without resorting to IOUs and script. Inspired by Walter's open business approach, general manager Frank Neely abolished the store's credit adjustment department and declared that anything a customer wanted to return would be taken back without question, and whatever the store could do to settle a complaint would be done, trusting that most of his customers were honest and decent people who would more than make up for whatever shady dealings he accepted. Sibley quoted one malcontent as saying, "Is this a store or a philanthropic institution?" The loyalty of its customer base and ever-expanding sales figures, however, proved the wisdom of Rich's policies.

Morris's grandson Richard took over the helm in 1947, expanding the store to multiple suburban locations to follow their migrating customer base, while sales at the main store continued to climb. Even with all this outlying growth, the downtown location did so well that Richard built a six-story home center across the street on Forsyth, with a four-floor "Crystal Bridge" joining the two. It was on this bridge, at the suggestion of his Design & Display Department head Frank Pallotta, that he initiated another beloved Atlanta tradition in 1948, the "lighting of the Great Tree." Every year, a large, sixty-to-seventy-foot-high white pine, cedar, or spruce tree was located somewhere in the Southeast, trucked to Atlanta in high ceremony, installed on top of the bridge, decorated with several thousand ornaments and lights, and then lit right after sunset on Thanksgiving night, accompanied by hundreds of choruses and performers. After the downtown Rich's closed in 1991, the tradition moved to the flag-ship suburban location at Lenox Square. In Atlanta, this tradition-ally starts the official Christmas shopping season, which unofficially seems to start around Labor Day!

Following the death of Richard Rich in 1975, his beloved store was bought by an out-of-town conglomerate, Federated Department Stores, which kept the name for a number of years, but never seemed to fully understand the mystique Rich's had gained among native Atlantans. Reversing the easy credit and liberal return policies to better match its other stores' hard-headed business approaches, the conglomerate's sales started declining almost immediately. Federated changed the name in 2003 in favor of what they thought was the more glamorous of their decidedly Northern-oriented holdings, Rich's-Macy's, and then dropped the beloved name Rich's entirely on March 6, 2005. One hundred thirty-eight years of Atlanta history, traditions, and treasured memories disappeared along with the logo that day.

The opening of a small mercantile shop in a tarpaper shack along a war-torn street seems such a trivial event in the grand sweep of history, but Rich's was more than just another store to generations of Atlanta families. It was a place that epitomized the best of what makes the South special and different: It was genteel, open, welcoming, friendly, a place you could trust, staffed with men and women who were more like distant relatives than disconnected clerks.

THE INVENTION OF COCA-COLA

1886

John Stith Pemberton was a number of things: a respected Confederate combat veteran, wounded in action; the nephew of one of the most celebrated Confederate generals; a former physician turned prominent formulaic pharmacist who harbored secret addictions to some of his own ingredients (as most pharmacists did at the time); a repeatedly failed businessman who reneged on his loans and cheated his partners; and a central figure in the postwar patent-medicine era. He is today remembered for none of these things, but celebrated as the inventor of the world's most popular soft drink, Coca-Cola. Of all his notorieties and accomplishments, however, this was the one thing that he had a less than exclusive role in producing.

When Pemberton arrived in postwar Atlanta in 1870, it was a study in contrasts, still badly damaged and rebuilding, with a massive, six-story-high grand hotel just opening, but most businesses still operating out of tents or hastily constructed, crude wooden buildings. The dirt streets were filled with carpetbagging Yankees out to make their fortune on Southern miseries, Union troops still occupying the

Southern stronghold, newly arrived eastern European immigrants, and former Confederate soldiers still rootless and malnourished. Pemberton had grown up just outside the west-central Georgia town of Columbus, and he was seriously wounded defending it in the last major fight of the Civil War in Georgia. Many of his fellow veterans still suffered years later from wounds and diseases brought on by the war, and the unregulated pharmaceutical industry ran wild with all sorts of dubious and unlikely, not to mention downright unhealthy and dangerous, products claiming to cure their ills, while lightening their wallets in equal measure.

Pemberton had received his first physician's license in 1850, when he was only nineteen, based on his medical and pharmaceutical studies of Samuel Thomson's theories at the Southern Botanico-Medical College in Macon, Georgia. The Thomsonian School, or Physiomedicalism as it became known later, emphasized the use of steam baths and stimulating herbal remedies to cause vomiting and other purges of "toxins," in the belief that restoring the body's "natural heat" would cure any illness. This became a very popular modality of treatment in the mid-nineteenth century, though it received nearly universal condemnation from conventional medical practitioners and led to the first attempts at government oversight and regulation of the field. Pemberton set up shop in the bustling epicenter of Atlanta soon after arriving, applying his training and years of experience in this form of herbology by producing a series of unlikely if essentially harmless patent medicines; some of his wares included Compound Extract of Stillingia, Triplex Liver Pills, and Globe Flower Cough Syrup. He soon gained status as a leading pharmacist, and the state of Georgia commissioned his laboratories for the testing of agricultural chemicals. He was also invited to become one of the founding members of the first licensing board for pharmacists in the state, furthering his reputation as one of the most prominent and respectable citizens of the city. But behind his kindly visage and friendly nature, Pemberton hid a terrible secret. Like many wounded veterans of the day, he was addicted to morphine.

Some of the most widely accepted "facts" about the Civil War are that there were no pain-relieving drugs for the wounded soldiers, that mangled arms and legs were hacked off without the use of anesthetics, and that hospitals were filled with dying soldiers shrieking their lungs out from pain. The truth is that with some isolated exceptions, anesthetics for surgery and analgesics for pain relief were readily available on both sides of the lines. Surgeons did indeed have to have several assistants to hold down the squirming wounded, but this was due to the hallucinogenic properties of the drugs used in surgery—wounded soldiers lashed out in a drug haze, not primarily from pain. Many veterans, Pemberton included, became seriously addicted to the easily available primary drug used for pain relief, morphine. This was not a problem isolated to the veterans of the American Civil War by any means; the seriously high addiction rates to morphine among the German veterans of the Franco-Prussian War of 1871 led to a number of companies hastily researching possible alternatives. One company, the Bayer Pharmaceutical Company of Elberfeld, Germany, came up with a synthetic version of an opiate analgesic, diamorphine, that they first believed had not only greater pain-relieving qualities than morphine but also possessed no addictive properties whatsoever. They first sold this wonder drug in 1898 as a cough suppressant and pain-relieving alternative for morphine under the trade name "Heroin."

Many, if not most, of Pemberton's formulaic efforts were in this same vein, to find some less addictive, more effective product for the constant pain he and his fellow wounded veterans suffered from. A new drug on the market, cocaine, had received wide publicity in the mid-1880s after former president Ulysses Grant used it to soothe his cancerous throat. Pemberton had already been experimenting with the Peruvian paste, remarking that his own use of it "gave a sense of increased intelligence and a feeling as though the body was possessed of a new power." A popular French tonic, Vin Mariani (or Mariani's Wine), had arrived on the scene at about the same time, bearing both 7.2 milligrams of cocaine per fluid ounce and the heartfelt endorsements of soon-to-be-president William McKinley, Queen Victoria, Pope Leo XIII, and Thomas Edison. Pemberton hastily created his own barely modified version of the tonic, mixing the cocaine-based wine drink with a tiny amount of extract of the African kola nut, and naming it French Wine Cola. It was a nearly instant success, and to that time, the biggest seller of anything Pemberton had concocted. Pemberton remarked that he had sold a whopping 888 bottles on one memorable Saturday in 1885.

He had two problems, though. He needed capital, meaning another set of partners, and he had burned through too many in town to find another easily. In addition, his sales of the new product were hampered by a new prohibition movement that resulted in the city closing the doors of saloons, and a short-lived though widespread public tendency away from intoxicating beverages. Luckily, however, his French Wine sales would remain legally unchecked. His first problem was solved by the arrival of a pair of Union veterans, Frank Robinson and David Doe. Natives of Maine, they had invested everything they had and could borrow on a printing press and had headed to Atlanta to seek their fortune in the advertising business. They were soon recommended to Pemberton, and the three struck up an agreement to share the profits under a new corporation, the Pemberton Chemical Company. Robinson had been formally trained as an accountant, and he possessed a keen eye for business that Pemberton most decidedly lacked. He also had his eye on a new product line that had nothing to do with Pemberton's analgesical obsessions: soft drinks.

Atlanta in the pre-air-conditioning era was notable for one thing in the summer, the blindingly oppressive heat that permeated every part of life in the city. Five newfangled soda fountains had opened in the city, and Robinson convinced Pemberton that they should produce a soft drink to sell through the fountains. Their French Wine Cola was still a best seller, primarily among the sick and weak, but at $1 per bottle it couldn't compete with the 5-cent fountain drinks Atlantans were beginning to embrace with gusto. Pemberton was still enamored of the kola nut, another new drug that had arrived in 1881 accompanied by curative tidings as prominent as those of cocaine. He had difficulties, however, in figuring out how to use it in a recreational drink. The active ingredient in kola nuts is caffeine, which in liquid extract form has a bitter and unpleasant bite. This is perfectly acceptable in something taken as a medication or tonic, as French Wine Cola was advertised to be, but ran counter to what the public was seeking in a light, pleasant relief from the heat.

Agreeing to the venture, Pemberton spent most of the spring of 1886 in his basement laboratory, frequently joined by Robinson, trying to concoct some method of making a cold, caffeine-based beverage that would be palatable. He finally succeeded by reducing the bitter kola extract to a minimal drop, adding a German-produced synthetic caffeine to create the desired "kick" while eliminating the bitterness. To the mixture he added large amounts of sugar as a stimulant, caramel to give the drink a dark appearance (which helped hide any impurities, a common practice in the patent-medicine era), fruit juices and mild acids to balance the sugar-sweetness, and extract of coca leaves as an added stimulant. This gave the resulting syrup a small if measurable amount of cocaine, along with about four times the amount of caffeine in today's product, a stimulating drink indeed!

Willis Venable, the "Soda Water King of the South," operated one of the largest soda fountains in the South inside Jacob's Pharmacy, just three blocks away from Pemberton's laboratory. He agreed to help him "tweak" the formula. By late May 1886, a suitable balance of ingredients was at last produced, and at Robinson's suggestion, the new drink was named Coca-Cola. Robinson worked closely with a local engraver, Frank Ridge, on a trademark logo for the product, and soon had the familiar script produced and distributed on flyers all over town. A born advertising man, Robinson arranged for promotional endorsements from prominent citizens, gave out coupons for free drink samples, and hung advertising notices on every available space he could find, including the sides of streetcars.

Just as the new drink started to become popular, Pemberton fell seriously ill, prompting the newly formed corporation to flounder and David Doe to pull out completely. Robinson did everything in his power to continue the advertising and promotion blitz, but from his sickbed, Pemberton applied to the U.S. Patent Office on June 6, 1887, to register "Coca-Cola Syrup & Extract," but only in his own name, not the name of his partnership corporation. Broke as usual, and needing money to settle his last affairs, Pemberton reformed the business without notifying Robinson, giving the priceless formula to Venable and George Lowndes, an old friend from the patent-medicine days. Without ever leaving his sickbed, having spent what little he eventually received from Venable and Lowndes, Pemberton died penniless on August 16, 1888.

Robinson, the man who had come up with the concept for the soft drink, helped develop the formula, designed the trademark logo, and led the first attempts to advertise the product, the one who was the real force behind the Real Thing, was initially left out in the cold. Just before Pemberton's death, however, he was restored to control of the company, when a prominent local businessman, Asa Candler, obtained Pemberton's share by canceling yet another loan he had made to him, paying off the remaining partners, and putting Robinson in charge of placing the product back on the market. Under Candler's control, the formula was tweaked once again, any traces of both the coca leaf and the kola nut were removed, and the drink the world knows today was born. Ironically, Pemberton is noted both in popular memory and in the company's archives as the inventor of the refreshing beverage, although he had to be talked into producing the formula instead of working on his true interests, had little or nothing to do with the production and distribution of it, died shortly after developing the original formula, and sold it out from under his partner, who had in fact been almost solely responsible for its success.

THE COTTON STATES AND INTERNATIONAL EXPOSITION

1895

If one non–Civil War event can be said to best define the character of the city of Atlanta, it is the one hundred–day-long Cotton States and International Exposition. The United States had come to a sort of crossroads at this time, thirty years after the end of the Civil War, and stood on the brink of becoming an international power in the model of the European nations that had colonized her. In Atlanta, race relations had settled down after the stormy Reconstruction era, local businesses were beginning to attract national and international attention, agricultural production had been restored and now soared above prewar levels, and the leading citizens of the burgeoning city were anxious to cast aside its battle-torn image in favor of one devoted to progress and business. The Cotton States and International Exposition was the event that stood at the end of one war and the beginning of another.

Since the end of the Civil War, two things have epitomized Atlanta in the national scope: It is a hub of transportation for the nation, and to a lesser degree the western world, and it relentlessly promotes itself politically and commercially as the viable and productive heart and soul of the New South. A great deal of this self-promotion began with the work of a prominent editor of the *Atlanta Constitution* newspaper in the 1880s, Henry Grady. Grady, who never held an elected office or founded a single business, nevertheless saw his position as a bully pulpit for the promotion of Progressive Democratic social and political programs of his era, as well as himself as a spokesman for the growing commercial interests in the city, state, and region.

Grady made his national reputation in an impromptu 1886 speech in New York City, when he was invited by the New England Society of New York, a lineage society and charitable organization, to speak at their annual banquet at the famed Delmonico's Restaurant. Surprised by the presence of former General William T. Sherman, who was showered with cheers when introduced, and already nervous over the fact that he was present to give the "New South" response in a toast to a speech celebrating the Union victory in Atlanta by Thomas DeWitt Talmage, Grady rose to the occasion with an inspiring off-the-cuff speech. He first acknowledged Sherman's presence, remarking that he had been "kind of careless about fire," but proposed that Sherman's destruction had been a boon to the city, as it rose "from the ashes he left us in 1864" to a new, brave, and beautiful city of industry and commerce. He acknowledged the deep sacrifices made by both Union and Confederate soldiers, and the higher purpose these gave to the ground beneath the rebuilding city, hallowed by "the blood of your brothers who died for your victory, and doubly hallowed to us by the blood of those who died hopeless, but undaunted, in defeat." He closed by predicting that the newly industrious South would prove a worthy challenger to Northern commerce, and invited the two sides to join together in building a greater nation. "We have learned that one Northern immigrant is worth fifty foreigners and have smoothed the path Southward, wiped out the place where the Mason and Dixon's line used to be, and hung out the latchstring to you and yours."

Grady's speech was widely celebrated across the country, and city leaders moved quickly to seize upon the "New South" motif. Atlanta had hosted its first "international" exposition in 1881, a small affair in Oglethorpe Park that was centered on a display of cotton plants and products from around the world, but in 1887, with the push given by Grady's speech, it sought to make its mark with a larger and more elaborate exposition. The Piedmont Exposition opened on October 10 that year, in a newly cleared, 189-acre forest today known as Piedmont Park. Slightly larger in scope than the 1881 exposition, it featured several buildings exhibiting the scope of industry and agricultural development across the Southeastern region, and was perhaps most noted for hosting the first visit to Atlanta by a sitting president, Grover Cleveland. Although it was not a financial success, since few visitors attended over the 104-day stretch, with almost a fourth of the total number of exposition attendees present on the one day that Cleveland arrived, it did prove to business leaders and financial backers that the city government and commercial interests were able to work together successfully on such a venture.

A far larger and more expansive fair opened on September 18, 1895, the Cotton States and International Exposition. The hundred-day fair was primarily aimed at exploiting the growing relationships between the cotton-producing states in the Deep South and South American nations such as Argentina. Piedmont Park was chosen as the site again and underwent a phenomenally expensive transformation. Two million dollars ($50.9 million in today's dollars) was spent to upgrade and improve the old facilities, including the addition of a massive American pavilion, seventeen other major buildings, dozens of individual pavilions, "Tropical Gardens" (now known as the Atlanta Botanical Gardens), and the creation of an eleven-and-a-half-acre lake, complete with a boathouse and paddleboats for visitors, all designed by the English landscape architect, Joseph Forsyth Johnson. The Liberty Bell was brought down by rail from Philadelphia and housed in Pennsylvania's pavilion, and special "villages" of Sioux Indians, Chinese, Egyptians, and Mexicans graced the midway. A special establishment was the "Negro Building," intended to highlight both the culture and art of the black community, as well as their rise from slavery to productive citizenry in such a compressed amount of time.

In the midst of all these glittering, Gilded-Age displays of progress and innovation, two events underscored both where Atlanta had been and where it was heading. On the opening day, famed African-American educator Booker T. Washington was invited to make a speech. The first black person to be invited to such a prominent Southern platform, the ex-slave created a defining moment in civil rights history with his "Atlanta Compromise" speech. Comparing the plight of freedmen to sailors cast adrift on a massive freshwater river, he implored blacks to "cast down their buckets" for the salvation that already lay all around them. He rejected more radical ideas already circulating and urged his fellow ex-slaves to seek redemption and acceptance in Southern society, not through court challenges or by violent force, but through hard work in low-ranking roles in agriculture and industry. Wildly applauded by the audience, Washington was hailed as "the first Negro to ever electrify a predominantly white Southern audience." He was not widely hailed, though, by the black audience. Rejecting the "Atlanta Compromise" as one that would grant some temporary peace, but that would lead to a new form of economic slavery, Harvard-trained educator and activist William Edward Burghardt (W.E.B.) Du Bois later cofounded the National Association for the Advancement of Colored People (NAACP) to serve as a platform to actively resist any and all forms of segregation and discrimination. Washington's call for quiet assimilation and acceptance of political status was intended to reach the same goals as Du Bois' plan, albeit at a much slower pace. He hoped that this assimilation would cause a greater acceptance for blacks among the white power structures of the South, but his ideas ended up providing moral support for Jim Crow "separate but equal" policies, and setting racial progress in the South back by nearly a century.

While the war for civil rights entered a new phase at the exposition, another war came to a quieter conclusion. A few years after the Civil War ended, veterans from both sides formed fraternal organizations to keep up the close friendships they had developed during those terrible years of combat. The Grand Army of the Republic in the North started holding yearly reunions just a year after the war ended, followed by the United Confederate Veterans in the South in 1875; these groups were strictly segregated from each other at first. In July 1887, however, following two much smaller joint reunions, 200 ex-Confederates traveled to Gettysburg, Pennsylvania, to hold the first large reunion of the Blue and Gray. A highlight, on July 3, was a "charge" up Cemetery Ridge by a few survivors of Lee's Army of Northern Virginia, who again met up with their Union foes at the fence on top, this time to reach over and shake hands in joined brotherhood.

Eight years later, a thousand Union veterans from twenty-two states traveled to the Deep South for the first time since the war, joining thousands of Confederate veterans in Chattanooga from September 18 to September 20 to commemorate that divided victory there in 1863. Most of these veterans traveled together afterward to encamp at the Atlanta exposition, marching alongside each other to a joint campground inside the park on September 21. To the strains of specially composed martial music by John Philip Sousa and other prominent band leaders of the day, they made a mute declaration by their joint presence that the wounds that had torn the nation apart in 1861 were at last healed.

RACE RIOTS AND AUBURN AVENUE

1906

In the early years of the twentieth century, Atlanta had become nearly a boom town for trade and commerce. The city's population had swelled dramatically in the years following the Cotton Exposition, from just under eighty-nine thousand in 1900 to well over one hundred fifty thousand just ten years later. Thanks in large part to exposure from the three late-nineteenth-century expositions, Atlanta had gained a national and international reputation as a good place for business, a reputation that extended across the spectrum of race and cultures. However, this rapid expansion of wealth, business, and population led to one of the deadliest outbreaks of violence since Sherman had marched through, the 1906 Race Riots.

Although city and business leaders worked hard to project Atlanta's image as one of Southern gentility, harmony, and quiet productivity, there were a number of serious social stresses simmering underneath the polite surface. Although the combat phase of the Civil War had been over for forty years, the city had been occupied by federal troops and Northern political controllers for twelve more years and still had a strong core of residents who had lived through the Northern wrath, retribution, and humiliations afterward. The countryside was still dotted with "Sherman's Sentinels," fire-blackened chimneys standing as reminders of the large number of plantations and houses burned to ashes during the Union marches through Georgia. Postwar economic booms had been interrupted repeatedly by economic recessions and bank panics, resulting in great unease about the stability of the dollar, the security of savings and investments, and the outlook for continued employment at any given time.

To add to the general restlessness, there was still a great animosity toward the black population, and this was not relegated to the Deep South by any stretch. Veterans of both the Union and the Confederacy by and large blamed blacks for the wholesale slaughter of white soldiers, though this attitude had grown more muted as the years went on. Aside from a relative handful of radical abolitionists before the war, there were few who called for the inclusion of blacks into general society. Even the "Great Emancipator" himself, Abraham Lincoln, did not believe in such a multiracial society and had given funds to the "Return to Africa" movement intended to resettle former slaves in the new African nation of Liberia. Former slaves, caught between such widespread hostility and their natural desire for a normal, productive, and peaceful life, had largely stayed close to their former occupations on farms and plantations, working in slight modification of their former status through sharecropping and tenant farming, something that their Northern emancipators viewed with indifference at best. Ironically, in the midst of such harsh racial attitudes, the South was far more integrated and "multicultural" than the presumably more enlightened North. In antebellum times, blacks and whites grew up and worked together in close, nearly familiar relationships, although the racial disparities were always present if unspoken. The general idea of huge plantations worked by thousands of black slaves, with white owners mostly absent was not typical at all; the vast majority of slave owners, which at the peak constituted about 3 percent of the population, owned fewer than ten slaves and worked directly alongside them in the fields. On the other end of the spectrum, Lincoln's issuance of the Emancipation Proclamation in 1863 not only did not free a single slave but also caused widespread dissention, desertion, and even riots among Northern troops, many of whom were enraged that their mission to save the Union had been turned into a crusade to end slavery. It could accurately be said that not only in antebellum times but also well into modern times Southerners generally viewed blacks favorably as individuals but feared them as a class of people, while Northerners took the exact opposite viewpoint.

Fear of the millions of freed blacks had resulted in the formation of a number of terrorist organizations in the South following the war, the most notorious being the Ku Klux Klan. The most violent actions against emancipated blacks had been harshly put down by occupying Union troops during the Reconstruction Era, but the antipathy remained simmering under the surface long afterward. In Atlanta, black businessmen such as Alonzo Herndon, who made millions from his barbershop and insurance businesses, had begun prospering by the late 1870s and had developed homogeneous social, business, and educational institutions separate from white-dominated power structures, leading to more tensions in the rapidly growing city. Many whites felt that such prosperous blacks were "uppity," threats to the general social harmony in the city, and, perhaps more to the point, proving to be too effective as business competitors.

A last and ultimately fatal element contributing to the growing social tensions was the presence of large numbers of unemployed blacks and whites, who had flocked to the city from the poverty-stricken countryside, looking to profit in the booming business economy. The supply of newly arrived workers vastly outstripped the availability of jobs and led to more tensions between the races in the competition for the few available. The jobless blacks tended to gather in rows of low-end, dank saloons along Decatur Street, which rapidly (and not completely unfairly) gained a reputation as a dangerous part of town. Newspapers of the day soon carried front-page, lurid stories of murder and mayhem that were equal parts fact and fiction, the standards of journalism being no better then than they are today. Prosperous black businessmen were connected in the public's mind to the violence of the Decatur Street underclass, though they sought to distance themselves as much as possible from these undesirables. By the turn of the century, the general atmosphere of racial hatred and fear was a bomb waiting to explode, needing only a spark to ignite real violence. This spark came in the form of the 1906 campaign for Georgia's new governor.

The two leading gubernatorial candidates were the Democrats Hoke Smith and Clark Howell, Republicans being absent from state leadership until 2002. Both men were newspapermen by profession, Smith the former owner of the *Atlanta Journal*, and Howell the editor in chief and owner of the *Atlanta Constitution*. Both men seized upon the "Negro problem" in lieu of discussing much more complicated and divisive financial policy issues. Smith was a former cabinet official for President Cleveland, who had heartily endorsed Cleveland's "sound money" policies when the more expansive "free silver" policies of rival William Jennings Bryan played much better in the Southern state. Both men tried to outdo each other during the race by calling for more political and social restraints on the black population, Smith going so far as to call for a Constitutional amendment to disenfranchise blacks. Clark heartily agreed with the sentiment, but claimed, accurately, that strengthening the "white primary" system would gain the same result with less possibility of outside, meaning "Northern," outrage. Both men called for the repeal of the 15th Amendment and claimed that with the continued vote of blacks, who were the majority of the population in fifty-nine counties by 1900, whites would soon be ruled over and savagely put down by their former slaves. Both newspapers sought to strengthen their man's position by emphasizing every outrage by any black person, undoubtedly completely manufacturing at least some of them, and demanding in front-page, highlighted editorials that steps be taken to rein in the "black brutes."

The last straw came on the Saturday afternoon of September 22, 1906, when all the Atlanta papers carried huge banner front-page stories claiming that there had been a series of rapes and molestations of white women by black men the day before, none of which were ever proven. The city exploded in violence. By nine o'clock that evening, there was an armed mob of over ten thousand whites storming down Decatur Street, smashing the windows of black-owned businesses, dragging black men, women, and children out into the street and beating them, even stopping streetcars to drag off and beat black riders. Mayor James G. Woodward and other white leaders rushed to the scene trying to avert the violence, but to no avail. The State Militia was called out at around midnight, but the riots did not end until around two a.m., when a heavy rain began to fall.

On Sunday, September 23, even though newspapers carried the story that all blacks were now off the streets, hiding from the mob violence, white vigilante groups swept through the black sections of town, undeterred by the heavy presence of both military troops and city police. There is some credible evidence that at least some of the soldiers and officers either joined the mobs, or at the very least, discreetly looked the other way while they carried out their evil deeds. Violence continued on Monday, when a large group of blacks in Brownville were found to have armed themselves against further attacks; one policeman was killed in a subsequent raid on their stronghold. Shocked by the extreme violence they themselves had helped to begin, newspapers joined with city leaders and clergy on September 24 and 25 to plead for the mob violence to end. With the exception of scattered acts of vigilantism that went on for several more weeks, the race riots were over by Wednesday, September 26. The final toll is hard to calculate, as sources give wildly differing totals, but at least ten blacks and two whites were killed, and at least seventy people were injured. There was also massive damage to the Decatur Street business district.

Atlanta was permanently affected by the riots in one way: Most black businesses that had been formerly scattered throughout the city relocated along Auburn Avenue on the east side, which ended up becoming both a black-owned business mecca and the center of the later civil rights movement at the Avenue's Ebenezer Baptist Church. Black residents were "urged" to resettle in the Old 4th Ward near Auburn Avenue, and in the West End neighborhood, well away from areas of white business and social power structures. The Atlanta riots helped fuel regional segregation efforts, leading to increased Jim Crow legislation and helping the resurgence of the Ku Klux Klan and other white-power terrorist organizations.

THE FIRST FLIGHT IN ATLANTA

1910

The pace of life in Atlanta had, for all practical purposes, changed little in the forty-five years since the Civil War had ended. In 1910 horse-drawn carriages were still the primary method of transportation inside the city, the railroads still dominated the local economy, and the pace of life went no faster than a man could walk or a horse could trot. Electric-powered streetcars provided some small measure of public transportation, but just 30 percent of the streets were paved, while great attention was paid to the much more extensive system of paved and maintained sidewalks. The city was, however, standing on the cusp of an explosive period of growth, both in physical size and in pace of life, which would continue nearly unabated for the rest of the century. This growth was largely driven by two inventions, the automobile and the airplane.

Automobiles have a fuzzy history in Atlanta; the records are very unclear, but the man generally recognized as having the first one in the city was a bicycle dealer named William D. Alexander. In 1901 (or perhaps in 1897) he purchased three steam-power

"Locomobiles" that came as kits to be assembled. His first two-mile trip in one took him nearly two hours to complete, despite the total lack of rush-hour traffic, but proved an almost immediate hit. By 1910 there were thirty-five car dealerships in the city to serve the relatively small numbers of the population that could afford one. These pioneering car owners did have much in the way of political clout, though, and pushed the city council to fund a rapid paving program for the city streets. Ironically, this project has never been completed, in one of the most car-centric cities in America; as of 2007, there were still about twenty miles of dirt roads inside the city limits! Due to their staggering costs, cars were slow to catch on with the general public, but along with the extension of commuter lines by the Atlanta and Edgewood Street Railway Company, they helped fuel the expansion of suburbs. By the 1980s, Atlanta had become a "donut city," with a ring of heavily populated and expanding suburbs straddling I-285, the Perimeter Highway about ten miles out from the city center, while the population of the inner city itself was in a steady decline.

The other invention that had even fewer Atlantans directly involved, but which did even more to fuel the city's growth, was the airplane. Aviation had a more compact history than previous transportation developments, and this was reflected in Atlanta's experience. In Atlanta it took just eighteen years to go from the very first powered flights to regular passenger service. The first sustained (e.g., no falls off a cliff) manned flights were made by the French Montgolfier brothers in their self-designed and self-built hot air balloon near Paris on November 21, 1783. The effort for heavier-than-air flight was more competitively intense, and the history much more obscured by poor documentation and outright lies. It now appears that John Joseph Montgomery was the first man to fly and survive uninjured in a heavier-than-air craft, a glider of his own design and construction, in San Diego, California, on August 28, 1883. The much better known Otto Lilienthal of Germany, on the other hand, is now credited with making the first safe, repeated glider flights, starting in 1891. Lilienthal is also noted in the records as being the "first man to be photographed in flight." Another, less credible claim, is made for George Cayley of England, who some assert flew in the first successful glider in 1853.

Powered, sustained, heavier-than-air flight was the final goal, and although for years a claim has been made for Samuel Pierpont Langley and his Aerodrome as the first true airplane, it did not have a successful flight until 1914 (in a seriously modified version), crashing both times in its 1903 attempts. His main claim to this fame is the fact that both the U.S. War Department and the Smithsonian Institution had funded his experiments, and quite understandably, wanted something out of them. Gustave Whitehead claimed to have made a powered flight in Pittsburgh in 1899, adding that he crashed into a three-story building while distracted by stoking the steam engine, but no one else on the scene seemed to have noticed the alleged flight. The Wright brothers, Orville and Wilbur, are generally recognized as finally completing the first manned, powered, sustained, heavier-than-air flight, in their Flyer over Kill Devil Hill, North Carolina, on December 17, 1903.

Ben Epps of Athens was the first aviator in Georgia, flying his self-designed and self-built aircraft for the first time on August 29, 1909, "skimming the ground" in a flight of only fifty yards. Atlanta's first exposure to aviation was just eight months later on the afternoon of May 2, 1910, when Charles K. Hamilton, the "Man-Bird" as the local papers dubbed him, demonstrated his Glenn Curtiss–built Aeroplane at the Candler racetrack in front of a moderate-size crowd there to witness not his flight but the new sport of automobile racing. In one of the hallmarks of early aviation, Hamilton raced around the track against a Fiat automobile driven by Ralph De Palma, the car winning the race around the two-mile oval.

This first "air show" had a great impact on the public, even though the aircraft themselves were the crudest and most fragile of devices, and the science of aeronautics was not very well developed. One newspaper article claimed, "Atlanta has a natural altitude of 1,100 feet above sea level. With atmospheric conditions of this nature, it is difficult to glide the plane upward, as the lighter atmosphere is more difficult to navigate." Another reporter remarked that "air travel is no longer impracticable, and that the time is not far off when the automobile will be put in the discard for the flying machine, just like the horse we passed up for the automobile." Aviation was generally considered a simple novelty, though, until the significant use of aircraft in World War I showed one potential use for them, and postwar airmail routes paid for by the federal government showed another, more commercially lucrative use.

With the public's interest in the new devices growing, City Alderman William B. Hartsfield, an early aviation proponent, sought out an appropriate site for a landing field, and settled on the abandoned racetrack south of the city center, the same one Hamilton had flown over just sixteen years previously. On Thursday, April 15, 1925, Atlanta Mayor Walter Sims signed a simple agreement without ceremony to lease a 287-acre plot of land around the property south of the downtown area. This five-year lease was to establish Atlanta's first dedicated airfield, with the hopes that some minor airmail business might be attracted to the city. That evening, a small crowd of fifty aviation enthusiasts met at City Hall to organize a committee with plans to make Atlanta "the leading Air Port of Dixie." Atlanta was born as a transportation hub, not as a destination, and an airport was seen as the next logical step in its progression. What would become the busiest airport in the world started with this single lease agreement and meeting. Soon named after the former owners, the Asa Candler family of Coca-Cola fame, Candler Field provided a relatively smooth and large open place to allow the slow aircraft of the day adequate space to land and take off without paved runways or much in the way of infrastructure.

The first commercial use of the new airport was on September 15, 1926, when the equally new Florida Airways inaugurated their Atlanta to Miami airmail route, with stops (or at least dropped deliveries) at Macon, Jacksonville, Tampa, and Fort Myers along the way. This business proved to be short-lived, with the last route flown on December 26. It cost ten cents per ounce to deliver a first-class letter via airmail, while it cost two cents per ounce for regular ground delivery. The field languished until May 1, 1928, when the first regularly scheduled air service company, Pitcairn Aviation, later known as Eastern Airlines, opened business at Candler Field. Business picked up quickly, and on April 13, 1929, the city bought the property outright for $94,400 ($1.2 million in 2009 dollars), changing the name of the field to the Atlanta Municipal Airport.

Regularly scheduled passenger service from the Atlanta airport was inaugurated on October 15, 1930, by American Airlines, offering regular flights to Dallas and Los Angeles. In 1934, another Atlanta icon arrived at the field, when a former crop-dusting and failed passenger airline out of Monroe, Louisiana, gained the government mail contract route from Dallas to Charleston, with a stopover in Atlanta. Delta Air Corporation, later Delta Airlines, resumed their passenger service along with the mail route that same year, flying a small fleet of Stinson Trimotors to several southeastern cities.

At that first Atlanta airport meeting on April 15, 1925, two prophetical speeches were offered. Carl Hutchison, the newly elected secretary of the airport committee, "predicted that within a few years the air would be full of airplanes connecting every important city."

Atlanta attorney Harry McGriff offered another vision. Recalling the somewhat peripheral use of aircraft in the recent Great War (World War I), he predicted that aircraft would become the primary means of both offense and defense in any future wars. Just fourteen years later, McGriff's vision came to fruition with the German blitzkrieg attacks during World War II. Hutchinson's vision took longer to be realized. Renamed the William B. Hartsfield Atlanta International Airport in 1977, and renamed again the Hartsfield–Jackson Atlanta International Airport in 2003, the airport became the busiest in the world in 1999. By 2009 it had over 970,000 flights and eighty-eight million passengers per year.

THE MET ARRIVES IN ATLANTA

1910

Promptly at eight o'clock p.m. on the evening of Monday, May 2, 1910, the lights dimmed at the new and cavernous Atlanta Auditorium-Armory, the hubbub of conversation among Atlanta's glitterati subdued, conductor Albert Hertz raised his baton, and the overture to Richard Wagner's *Lohengrin* began. As the curtain rose, King Heinrich was revealed, sitting under the Judgment Oak on the banks of the Scheldt River near Antwerp. A herald stepped forward, singing:

> *Hört! Grafen, Edle, Freie von Brabant!*
> *Heinrich, der Deutschen König, kam zur Statt,*
> *mit euch zu dingen nach des Reiches Recht.*
> *Gebt ihr nun Fried und Folge dem Gebot?*

> *(Hear ye, counts, nobles and freemen of Brabant!*
> *Heinrich, King of the Germans, has come to this place*

to confer with you according to the law of the realm.
Do you willingly obey his command?)

The grandest of grand opera, in the form of the famed Metropolitan Opera Company of New York, had arrived in Atlanta.

Atlanta was not an obvious location for such high spectacle, born as a muddy backwater terminal station for an obscure rail line in the Southern wilderness, nearly totally destroyed by war only fifty years previously, and still not completely recovered economically or socially from the experience. It did, however, have a surprisingly long history of opera and other high art performances, beginning just over a year after the Civil War ended, well before any significant part of the city had been rebuilt.

Two businessmen, S. H. Hubbard and A. J. Nelson, rented space in the rebuilt Bell & Johnson Building in July 1866, intending to bring Shakespearian theater to the hall by that fall. Instead, on October 18, Max Strakosch and his Italian Ghioni and Sussini Grand Opera Troupe presented the very first production of opera in Atlanta, Verdi's *Il trovatore.* It must have been quite a hit, as this full opera was followed by two more complete performances in the following two evenings, Bellini's *Norma,* and Rossini's *Il barbiere di Siviglia.* Ghioni and Sussini had a rather large cast for the time, over seventy-five musicians and singers, including Strakosch's wife Amalia Patti Strakosch, the prima donna.

Operas at that time were noted for having their librettos "adjusted" to suit their audiences, and Strakosch used the practice, and his well-known wife, to help drum up more business from what he presumed were largely unsophisticated Scottish and Irish inhabitants of the city. A note in the *Atlanta Intelligencer* on October 21 mentioned that "Madam Patti will surely sing all three of her famous Irish songs, because the audience will stop the show until she sings

'Comin' Through the Rye.'" This popular tune, along with "Within a Mile of Edinboro Town" and "Kathleen Mavoureen," took the place of Rossini's short operatic arias during the "singing lesson" scene in Act II.

These performances were followed in short order by the openings of two other opera companies, the high art proving a hit in the city. By 1870, the Belgian consul to Atlanta, Laurent DeGive, was moved to create his own larger and more ornate facility, DeGive's Opera House opening in 1870 at the corner of Marietta and Forsyth Streets. It was enlarged just three years later to nearly double its capacity to a total of two thousand seats. Atlanta's total population was only twenty-eight thousand that year!

In the mid-nineteenth century, Italian opera was all the rage in Europe, the practice spreading to Atlanta and its Eurocentric society mavens. It wasn't until 1877 that an opera in another language made its way to the Atlanta stage, Julius Eichberg's English opera, *The Doctor of Alcantar*. Gilbert & Sullivan's *H.M.S. Pinafore* followed two years later, the very model of a modern popular opera, and a wild favorite of crowds that sold out every performance. More glittering opera houses were constructed in Atlanta and the surrounding area during the late part of the century to provide for the growing operatic taste; DeGive himself built a second grand house at 157 Peachtree Street (which later became Loew's Grand Theater).

Opera and other classical music performances grew increasingly popular in Atlanta through the late nineteenth century. Three organizations were formed to fund their presentations; the Mozart Club, the Beethoven Society, and the Rossini Club were all patronized by the increasingly well-heeled, upper-crust society of the city. In 1905 the three combined their funding to present the first Atlanta Music Festival, followed by repeat festivals in 1907 and 1909, which brought in the very best operatic singers, musicians, and orchestras from around the nation and Europe. The famed Metropolitan Opera soprano Geraldine Farrar sang her arias from that year's hit *Madame Butterfly* at the 1909 festival and later suggested to its directors that they attempt to bring the entire troupe to the city. One of the administrators of the Met was also in town, Ernest Goerlitz, and enthusiastically seconded Farrar's suggestion. Farrar no doubt put pressure on her close friend, and rumored lover, the internationally famed tenor Enrico Caruso, to help pressure the troupe's management to bring them South.

The Met responded positively and agreed to come down for the 1910 season with the condition that Atlanta guarantee box office receipts of at least $40,000. This amount was raised within a few weeks by some two hundred of the leading citizens, organizations, and businesses in town eager to host such a prestigious event. The opening night, eagerly anticipated for weeks, was far and away the most ornate, glittering spectacle of wealth and glamour the young city had ever before beheld. The well-received *Lohengrin* was followed on Tuesday night by *Tosca*, conducted by Egisto Tango. Then on Wednesday, May 3, Caruso made his Southern debut as Radames in *Aida*, conducted by Fernando Tanara. This drew the largest crowd he had ever performed to up until that time, a paid admission of 7,042.

Madame Butterfly was presented under conductor Vittori Podesti on Thursday night, followed by *Hansel und Gretel* under Hertz on Friday, May 5. Caruso returned to the stage to great acclaim as Canio in *Pagliacci*, under conductor Tango, on the closing night performance that Saturday. Total receipts for the week of concerts topped $71,000 and paid attendance of twenty-seven thousand was a record for the company. The Met's box office manager, Max Hirsch, told a reporter for the *Atlanta Constitution*, "Never before had the Metropolitan Opera Company sung to so many people or such an amount of money in one week, despite the fact that six or more performances are given in a week in New York."

Society notices in the Atlanta papers gushed over the ornate and colorful garb worn by the society mavens, much as certain television programs today excitedly broadcast details of starlets on red carpets. Tuesday morning's *Atlanta Constitution* dutifully reported that Mrs. William Lawson Peel, wife of the director, "wore a white brocade satin gown with overdress of white net embroidered in white and silver threads; the corsage finished with point lace." Not to be outdone, Mrs. Robert J. Lowery was outfitted in "a Parisian toilet [toilette] in soft rose-colored chiffon; the corsage was exquisite in combination with the rose-color and lace." These details filled up nearly a half-page of small type in both the morning (*Constitution*) and evening (*Journal*) newspapers all that week.

The Met officials somewhat reluctantly agreed to come South for the 1911 season, though they voiced the opinion that the 1910 performances had been a fluke and Atlanta was not really prepared to host annual performances. They could not have been more wrong. Box office receipt and attendance records broke those of the year before, even though only four operas were offered. By 1912, opera was so obviously well received in Atlanta, and the Met performances so well attended, that its managing director, Otto Kahn, proclaimed the city to be the company's second home:

> *Grand opera for the South in Atlanta is an established*
> *institution now, and in the future anyone who wishes*
> *to hear grand opera as given by the Metropolitan*
> *Company in America must either go to New York or*
> *Atlanta for it.*

The Met became a yearly event, interrupted only by the Great Depression and World War II, until in 1986 its famed orchestra and operatic stars graced an Atlanta stage for the last time.

THE LYNCHING OF LEO FRANK

1913

In the spring and summer of 1913, there were only two facts about a horrific crime that everyone could agree on; thirteen-year-old Mary Phagan was dead and she had died where she worked, a pencil factory in downtown Atlanta. Nearly everything else about the case was disputed, especially in the lurid details posted every day in the competing newspapers. One other fact was considered very significant to the case: Her former boss, Leo Max Frank, was Jewish.

Although the first Jewish settlers in Georgia arrived in Savannah shortly after James Oglethorpe had founded the colony, they remained a distinct minority all through the nineteenth century. The first Jewish residents of Atlanta were Jacob Haas and Henry Levi, who arrived in 1846 to set up mercantile businesses. During the Civil War years, there were only about fifty Jewish residents in the city. One of Haas's former employees, David Mayer, became a noted blockade-runner and member of Governor Joseph Brown's staff during the war; he was one of a surprisingly high number of prominent Jewish Confederate officers. After the war, a new influx of eastern European Jews entered the city, fleeing war and poverty in their home countries, and seeking freedom from persecution and pogroms in the collapsing Ottoman Empire.

Even with this new increase in the Jewish population, there was very little in the way of anti-Semitism in Atlanta throughout the nineteenth century, due in part to the prominent role Jews had in the business sector. Morris Rich, the founder of Rich's was Jewish, as well as Joe Jacobs, the owner of a chain of pharmacies that had been the birthplace of Coca-Cola. Jews were also noted for their even-handed extension of business and credit to both the white and the black communities, and for carving out enclaves in what had been predominantly black sections of town.

There was, however, notable anti-Semitism in the nation at large all through the late nineteenth century, increasing in both scope and intensity as larger waves of Jewish immigrants from eastern Europe arrived around the turn of the century. During the Civil War, both sides complained of profiteering and unfair business practices by Jewish merchants. Union General Ulysses S. Grant gained notoriety for issuing an order in 1862 banning Jews from his area of operations in western Tennessee, blaming them for running a "black market" in pilfered cotton and engaging in corrupt trade as sutlers to his army. The order was swiftly rescinded by higher authorities and came back to haunt Grant during his 1868 presidential bid, when there were calls by rabbis to vote against him for issuing the order. Grant publically repudiated the order during his campaign, claiming it had come from his superiors, and ended up carrying most of the Jewish vote that year.

During the 1880s and 1890s, Jews were part of a larger group of immigrants coming to America who experienced stiffer resistance from nativist groups. This resistance reached a peak during the 1896 presidential campaign, when the Populist Party accused the

Cleveland administration of selling bonds to several prominent Jewish financiers, including J. P. Morgan, "proving" that the government was in collusion with a shadowy "international Jewish conspiracy" to destroy the wealth of nations. This was part of a European-based growing anti-Semitic movement, which exploded later in the rise of the National Socialists in Germany. This movement in America did not go to those lengths, but did lead to a rise in job, housing, and social discrimination all through the first half of the twentieth century. By 1906, the situation had become worrisome enough to warrant the formation of the American Jewish Committee to safeguard and promote civil and legal rights of Jews in the United States.

Soon after graduating from Cornell University with a degree in mechanical engineering, eighteen-year-old Leo Frank, born in Texas but raised in Brooklyn, was invited by his uncle to join him at a factory in Atlanta he had just invested in, the National Pencil Company. Leo agreed and spent the next year in Germany learning the trade at Eberhard Faber in Nuremberg. In 1908 he returned to the United States and joined his uncle in Atlanta at the factory on South Forsyth Street in the downtown sector. He was soon introduced to the daughter of a prominent Jewish family, Lucille Selig, and they married in 1910. Frank was accepted by his employees and coworkers, but was not very popular on the society circuit, primarily due to the fact that he was an "outsider," Yankee industrialist in the rebuilt but still somewhat philosophically unreconstructed city. A small, thin man who never appeared to be completely healthy, he did do well enough socially in the small Jewish community to be elected president of the local chapter of B'nai B'rith.

Frank's employer, though, had attracted the wrath of a local tabloid newspaper, the *Atlanta Georgian,* which accused the locally owned establishment of hiring almost exclusively young female teenagers (implying but never stating that there was something nefarious about the practice), and paying them only an average of twelve cents an hour, less than a third of what Northern factory workers pulled in. Both of these practices were not unusual at all in the business climate of the day, but scandal does sell papers. The *Atlanta Georgian* had been a small but straightforward journalistic competitor to the established *Atlanta Constitution* when it began printing in 1906 with low circulation and with an editorial slant promoting Prohibition and attacking the convict-lease system then employed by the state. In 1912, though, "yellow journalism" king William Randolph Hearst bought the paper, quickly transforming it into a better-selling lurid gossip tabloid with somewhat looser standards of journalistic integrity, in the same model as Hearst's other papers.

One of Frank's employees was thirteen-year-old Mary Phagan, the youngest of four children, born four months after her father's death, and a native of Marietta, just north of Atlanta. She had worked in various factory jobs since she was ten, trying to help keep her family afloat. At the pencil factory, she was assigned to a machine that placed erasers into the pencil's metal band, on the second floor of the building, just a few steps away from Frank's office. She had been there less than a year when she had a rare Saturday holiday, April 26, 1913, Confederate Memorial Day. Just after noon she went to the factory to collect her wages, $1.20 for a single, ten-hour day of work; Frank himself handed over her pay as usual. No one noted if Phagan then left the factory, but Frank was still in his office when the night watchman, Newt Lee, came in early for his shift at around four in the afternoon. Frank left sometime before six o'clock, but no one noted him leaving either. At about three o'clock the following morning, Lee frantically telephoned the police, stating that he had just found a female body in the narrow, long, and dark basement of the factory.

What the policemen discovered horrified them. Mary's body was so covered with grime and soot from the floor of the basement that it was at first unclear what race she was. Her dress had been pulled up and some of her underwear torn off, a strip of which was wrapped around her neck under a seven-foot length of three-quarter-inch cord, which had been used to strangle her. Her face was battered and bruised, one or both cheeks were slashed, dried blood was coming out of both her mouth and ears, and some of her fingers had pulled out of joint, apparently in a struggle with her attacker. An autopsy would later reveal that her skull had been broken, and she had suffered bite marks on her shoulders; "strange violence" had been done to her sexual organs, though the report never concluded that she had been raped. There were many bloody fingerprints, stained doors, and a blood-stained metal bar found at the scene, none of which were subjected to any sort of testing (though this was in the very early days of forensic fingerprint analysis). Two mysterious, barely literate notes were also found at the scene, bearing inscriptions that seemed to point to the night watchman Lee as the guilty party.

At first the prime suspects were Lee himself, who the policemen at the scene described as "agitated," and a black janitor who worked in the building, Jim Conley. Conley and Lee were both questioned very intensely by the police, but claimed to have no part in or knowledge of the crime. Frank had been hustled out of bed at around four a.m., and the detectives who questioned him at the time thought it was suspicious that he seemed very nervous and forgetful, having a hard time getting his things together to go to the factory with them. Several other small issues like this seemed to cast a measure of doubt on Frank's innocence in the matter, at least in the minds of some investigators, but by far the great weight of physical and witness evidence eventually pointed straight at Conley as the perpetrator.

The *Atlanta Constitution* broke the story the morning of April 27, with a special edition hitting the streets minutes after Phagan's mother was given the grim news. This touched off a wild free-for-all

competition for headlines with the *Atlanta Georgian,* which put out
no less than forty special editions that first day. Frank soon became a
target of both papers, which carried increasingly anti-Semitic editorials against the "Yankee Jew" as the police investigation dragged on
through the month of May. The *Atlanta Georgian* eventually muted
its tone, responding to an outraged backlash from the Jewish community in town, but, strangely, also paid for an attorney to represent
Conley. The *Constitution,* though, continued with attacks against
Frank, mixed with loud complaints about how long the investigation
was taking.

On May 24, a grand jury returned a murder indictment against
Frank, and his trial began on July 28. Conley became the state's leading witness, retelling a story he had first told police investigators, of
how Frank had come to him for help in hiding the body of a girl he
had accidentally killed and had then dictated these mysterious notes
for him to write. He embellished the story on the witness stand,
adding that Frank frequently had sexual relations with women in his
factory office, while Conley served as a lookout for him. Defense witnesses showed the great holes in Conley's claims and the lack of any
physical evidence tying Frank to the crime should have ended the
case against him before it started, but the newspaper-driven public
outrage was too much for the jury to ignore. Frank was found guilty
on August 25, with a sentence of death. His initial appeals failed,
though Supreme Court Justice Oliver Wendell Holmes led an effort
to bring his case before the nation's highest court. This appeal, too,
failed at 7–2, with Holmes writing in his dissent, "Mob law does
not become due process of law by securing the assent of a terrorized
jury."

Doubt about Frank's guilt still existed, though further rage
against him was whipped up by the newspapers, joined this time by
newspaperman and local politician, Tom Watson, and his *Weekly*

Jeffersonian. Every legal appeal was met by howls of printed derision, with Watson leading the parade of abuse. In the midst of all this blood-lust sound and fury, Frank's lawyer made a final appeal to Georgia Governor John M. Slaton for a commutation of Frank's sentence to life in prison. Slaton held a new hearing, carefully reviewed the evidence, and finally convinced that Frank had not received a fair trial, commuted his sentence to life the day before his scheduled execution date. Slaton himself left office six days later, and though he had been a widely admired and respected governor, was forced to leave the state in the ensuing public outcry over his decision.

Watson redoubled his printed rage against Frank, openly calling for vigilantism. A group of prominent politicians, professionals, and lawmen in short order formed an open lynching society, the "Knights of Mary Phagan," advertising in the newspapers for handymen with the necessary skills to join them in "serving justice" to Frank. One of the ringleaders of the Knights was none other than two-term former Georgia governor Joseph M. Brown. On the afternoon of August 16, the group of twenty-eight men traveled to Milledgeville, took control of the state prison without meeting much, if any, resistance from the warden, seized Frank, and drove throughout the night back to Marietta. At seven a.m., a rope was thrown over the branch of a large oak tree, placed around Frank's neck, and he was turned to face in the direction of Phagan's house and hanged. A large crowd gathered to watch the proceedings, as evidenced by pictures on souvenir postcards that quickly became popular in the state.

The Knights of Mary Phagan did not disband after lynching Frank; they instead found another purpose under another name for the same sort of underground terrorism. They became the resurrected Ku Klux Klan.

THE KLAN REBORN

1915

On the windswept, chilly night of November 25, 1915, a group of men climbed the steep slope of Stone Mountain by flashlight, but only one was completely aware of what was to transpire. That night, a burning cross atop the rocky bald just east of downtown Atlanta, inspired by a movie sweeping the country, signaled a rebirth of part of the Old South and a path to further excesses by the Knights of Mary Phagan.

In the wreckage of the South after the Civil War, two significant forces arose. The first was a backhanded tribute to one of the truly great military leaders of this nation, Robert E. Lee, a man who did not believe in slavery as an institution and disapproved of ideas about secession, but who became the leader of one of the Confederacy's greatest armies. Lee was widely admired and respected on both sides of the conflict, to the point where he was accorded near-deification (which he angrily disapproved of). Trying to rationalize his military prowess with the righteousness of The Cause, however, combined with the ultimate Confederate loss proved a quandary for his admirers. This resulted in the rise of a quasi-religious movement known as the "Lost Cause" mythology, a Christological interpretation of Lee's role in the war in which Lee was given the role of the pure, saintly knight in pursuit of the correct and near-holy quest, but doomed to failure by both the sins of the people (not just in the practice of slavery) and the presence of evil, wicked Judases. His former corps commander and "right arm," James Longstreet, was accorded this latter role in the mindset of those believing in the mythology. The loss at Gettysburg had clearly doomed the South, but since Lee was in charge, a scapegoat had to be found. It did not matter that Longstreet had tried with all his might to talk Lee out of fighting there, and that Lee himself took full responsibility for the disaster even before the battle had ended. Longstreet had further cast himself into the pit by doing the unforgivable after the war—he became a Republican and willingly worked with the Reconstruction governments.

The second force that arose was originally intended to be a joke, a sarcastic take on then-popular "secret societies" like the Masons and Oddfellows by a group of highly educated, unemployed, and bored former Confederate officers in Pulaski, Tennessee. These men, John Lester, James Crowe, John Kennedy, Calvin Jones, Richard Reed, and Frank McCord, originally met in late 1865 in a law office and named their group the Ku Klux Klan (KKK), or "a band of family." (*Kuklos* is a Greek word meaning circle or band, and clan is an anglicized Scots Gaelic term for family or kinfolk.) In the mid-nineteenth century, it was considered humorous to misspell words that started with c by changing them to begin with k, which underscores the fact that the original intent of the group was comic. At first it confined its activities to collegiate-level practical jokes and general mischief fueled by not a little alcohol. It organized along military hierarchical lines and awarded grandiose titles in mockery of the Masonic custom—"wizard," "titan," "klegal," and so on. But in short order the small group took on a more serious tone.

The postwar South was not only wrecked economically and physically but also lacked any coherent political or legal structures as well. Small armed bands sprung up across the region, frequently consisting of well-trained and combat-hardened Confederate veterans, to protect citizens against violence from the large numbers of roaming, homeless, veterans and vagabonds. These groups also served to protect the white population from acts of vengeance or general violence from the millions of newly freed slaves, acts that proved to be more than simply rumors. Loosely organized groups of former slaves, called the Union League and Black Militias, did commit a large number of crimes and atrocities across the South in the first two years after the war, with the Union Reconstruction governments of the region often ignoring them and refusing to put them down with force. In response, white Southerners formed equally loosely organized bands for protection such as the Southern Cross, White League, and Knights of the White Camellia in Louisiana; the Red Shirts in the Carolinas and Mississippi; and dozens of "rifle clubs" and unnamed smaller groups in other states. In a very short of time, the KKK numbered among their ranks.

In its original incarnation, the Klan played a number of practical jokes on neighbors in the Pulaski area. One of its members' favorites was to dress up in white sheets and scare people by riding past their homes at night. Once it turned to a more serious purpose, it found this tactic worked well against the freed slaves in the area, who were threatened by the "ghosts of Confederate dead" coming back to haunt them. It also added more members, including former Confederate Brigadier General George Washington Gordon of Pulaski, who attempted to take the group to a new level. In 1867 he organized and led the first "national" meeting of the Klan in Nashville, where he presented his "Prescript" of formal organization and rules. Gordon was also instrumental in introducing former Confederate Major General Nathan Bedford Forrest to the Klan; he was soon proclaimed the "Grand Wizard," or national commander. Robert E. Lee himself was asked to join the group, but politely declined, citing his age and poor health.

In this early Reconstruction period, there were a tremendous number of outright acts of terrorism perpetrated against freed blacks and white Unionists, and because the Klan had adopted such a high, public profile in comparison to the other resistance groups, it was soon being blamed for every action that took place. It did not help that many of these other groups adopted the white-sheet costume, night-riding methods, and even the Klan name itself. From the very beginning, Forrest repudiated acts of terrorism and random violence, but maintained the Klan had a legitimate purpose in protecting the South from northern-affiliated terrorist groups, and in politically resisting the excesses of the Reconstruction government and Radical Republicans in Congress. He had no authority over the small, independent groups that had borrowed the name, and when the violence really began to get out of hand in 1869, he formally disbanded the KKK. There is some evidence he did this as part of a secret agreement with then-president Ulysses S. Grant, his former wartime foe, as a means of eliminating the possibility of true guerilla war breaking out and ending Reconstruction. Mostly out of respect for Forrest, membership gradually declined over the next two years, helped along by harsh federal legal and military attempts to quash the vigilante groups. By 1872 the Klan had essentially disappeared as a physical organization, if not as an idea.

Forty-three years later, on that freezing night atop Stone Mountain, William Joseph Simmons of Alabama resurrected the name of the Ku Klux Klan in a ceremony at the base of a large burning cross, this time as both a social fraternal order and as a political force to confront what many thought were the chief ills of the age. Among these was the widespread suspicion of Jews, which had come into national prominence with the trial and later lynching of Leo Frank. Several of the carefully selected men with Simmons that night had been members of the Knights of Mary Phagan, the very group that had abducted Leo Frank from his prison cell in August of that year and lynched him in Marietta. Two others were former members of the original Klan. Simmons had been deeply influenced by D. W. Griffith's blockbuster movie that had opened earlier in the year, *Birth of a Nation,* based on Thomas Dixon's 1905 novel, *The Clansman.* Dixon had deeply romanticized the actions and organization of the original Klan, equating the Southern Knights of the Klan with Sir Walter Scott's equally romanticized Scottish Highlanders. Both the film and Dixon's novel depicted the Klan's use of the symbols of a fiery cross and white robes with pointed hats, neither of which the original employed. The fiery cross had been a feature of life in the medieval Highlands, having been used by runners to gather widely scattered men to form armies for the clan chiefs. However, the Highlanders used the St. Andrews cross, as depicted on the Scottish national flag. Griffith and Simmons used the Christian Latin cross, instead, creating a quasi-religious ceremonial aspect around its burning.

Simmons's resurrection of the Klan had the same effect as the first appearance of the group had had; it rapidly spread, this time into the North and West as well as the South. The widespread popularity of the Klan can be seen in their annual marches down Pennsylvania Avenue in Washington, D.C., during the 1920s; twenty-five thousand white-robed Klansmen joined the march in 1926. It soon morphed into small, disparate bands that not only fought against black equality and Prohibition but also encouraged anti-Semitism and anti-Catholicism. This time, however, it conducted its affairs in the open and soon permeated so much of the politics of the South that one absolutely had to be a member in order to get elected to any office. This time, too, it lasted for far longer than the original, not being effectively shut down for another seventy years.

CUMBERLAND VS. GEORGIA TECH

1916

By the fall of 1916 Europe had been locked in a titanic world war for two years, which had long since dissolved into trench warfare that produced nothing but lengthy lists of casualties. Woodrow Wilson was president of the United States, engaged in lecturing to the European powers about his plans for peace and attempting to guide his own progressive political policies through a somewhat hostile Congress. But in Atlanta, at Georgia Tech, there was only one thing that mattered to Coach John Heisman—Cumberland University had humiliated his baseball team in the spring of that year, and he planned to return the favor with his phenomenal football team.

American football has a murky history; it is difficult to say exactly what it evolved from. Most likely it was a combination of Native American ball games (which later developed into field hockey and lacrosse) and variations of organized free-for-alls popular in some New England colleges, which were influenced by English-style rugby. Games resembling modern football began at the intercollegiate level shortly after the Civil War ended and developed into the modern game after several rules meetings. In 1882 the concept of downs and distance requirements were added. It was a brutal sport, featuring massed groups of linesmen arranged in wedge formation in order to crash through the opponent's lines, which, not infrequently, resulted in serious injury and even death. A rule change in 1888 allowed tackling below the waist, and the resulting carnage convinced players and coaches alike that some sort of protective padding was needed. Helmets were not added until the late 1890s, in a crude, barely adequate leather form that resembled pilot's helmets. These were not made mandatory at the college level until 1939.

Even with new protective pads and rule changes, the sport remained incredibly violent and lethal, to the point that then-president Theodore Roosevelt threatened to ban it outright in 1905, after nineteen players died in a single season. Rules committee meetings produced only two major changes, allowing the forward pass and outlawing mass formations, but these were sufficient to lower the carnage level while transforming the game into its modern form. It wasn't until 1912, though, that the core modern scoring system was developed, six points for a touchdown, one for an extra point, and three for a field goal.

Georgia Tech fielded its first team in 1892, the Engineers, eight years later hiring Heisman to coach both the football team and the baseball team. He was the first paid college football coach in history, earning $2,250 ($53,038 in 2009 dollars) and 30 percent of the home game receipts his first year. A native of Cleveland, and former player himself at Brown and the University of Pennsylvania, Heisman had previously coached for what became two of Tech's biggest rivals—the Agricultural and Mechanical College of Alabama (later known as Auburn University) from 1895 to 1899, and Clemson University from 1900 to 1903. Heisman's phenomenal 1903 Clemson squad beat Georgia Tech that year, 73-0. At Tech, Heisman started off with a winning season (8-1-1) and built up the program from that high plane, intending to take it to the national championship level. Tech, then as now, was well regarded as a superior academic institution, specializing in engineering programs, and attracting some of the finest scholars in the nation. Unlike today, scholarship was regarded as existing on a higher plane than athletics, and even the most hulking of student-athlete brutes regarded the former as more important than the latter. A winning coach like Heisman was able to attract the best of the lot, and by 1916, the Tech squad was noted for its massive size and raw power.

Cumberland had started its own football program in 1894, the Bulldogs, from its first year challenging the then-dominant powers in the sport: Vanderbilt University, the University of Alabama, Louisiana State University, and Georgia Tech. By 1903 the squad was good enough to win the Southern Championship, beating Heisman's Clemson team for the victory. Cumberland was a relatively small, but well-regarded private liberal arts school in Lebanon, Tennessee, which had rebuilt from its fiery destruction by Union cavalrymen during the Civil War, but had never quite regained its prewar status as a leading law school. Like many other small colleges scattered across the South, it struggled from time to time just to keep its doors open and its academic programs intact. Football was something decidedly optional, and the school dropped the program in 1906, resumed playing in 1912, dropped the program again in 1915, and then played a shortened program, including this one final game with Tech in 1916, before dropping the program for another three years.

A new president took charge of Cumberland in the spring of 1916, Dr. Homer Hill, who made the final decision to drop the football program for at least that year. George Allen, the newly appointed student manager for both the baseball and football teams, was told to write letters to each school already scheduled and cancel the games, but claimed that he overlooked Tech. Somehow, Heisman found out about the dropped football program, and contacted Allen, insisting that the game be played or that Cumberland would have to pay a forfeiture fee of $3,000 to Tech ($59,780 in 2009 dollars). Heisman had an ulterior motive; he expected to crush Cumberland, but what he was really looking to do was run up his total number of scored points for the year; in that era, the national championship was bestowed on the team with the most points, regardless of schedule. Heisman objected to the system, and by insisting Cumberland field a team, any team, he could make his point about the inanity of it.

Heisman was a lot of things, but a graceful loser was not one of them. On the train back from the disastrous baseball loss to Cumberland in the spring of 1916, he started his lengthy diatribe to his players with, "You flaming jackasses!" It went downhill from there for a goodly part of the trip back to Atlanta. When Allen contacted him, asking for mercy and pleading to be allowed to back out of their football contract, Heisman refused, but allegedly offered Allen a share of the demanded default payment as a reward for fielding a team that Tech could dutifully beat up on. Allen agreed, gained the reluctant support of Dr. Hill, and found fourteen men on campus willing to face the Goliaths of Tech. At least one player was a "ringer," a reporter from a Nashville newspaper who used a false name to gain admission to the squad, but it did not matter one little bit at the end. The outcome was never in doubt, the final score was the only issue in question.

Other than a rather dry play-by-play account in the *Atlanta Constitution,* it is very hard to separate fact from fiction about this historic game; it has most decidedly entered the realm of legend. Players on both sides embellished just about every possible aspect of the game over the years, and it doesn't help that the single published historical record is an amusing but entirely anecdotal book published sixty-seven years after the game, entitled *You Dropped It, You Pick It Up!,* by Jim Paul. It is true that Allen pleaded with Heisman without success to allow him to forfeit the game without the financial penalty, and then to at least shorten the game, preferably by thirty or forty-five minutes. Heisman, with the score standing at 126–0 at halftime, did allow the game to be shortened by a whole five minutes; however, he had more points to score on the field to underscore his views on the national championship decision. As Allen entered the Tech locker room to make his plea, he overheard Heisman telling his Engineers, "You are doing fine, men. We're ahead for now. But you just can't tell what those Cumberland players might have up their sleeves, they might spring a surprise. So be alert, men!" Allen knew there was no "trick" up his sleeve; his only concern was how to keep his players from leaving the field altogether.

At the end Georgia Tech stood atop the scoreboard with a phenomenal 222 points to zero for Cumberland. All this was done with not a single pass thrown by Tech, and neither side made even a single first down conversion (Tech scored every series and Cumberland never achieved even one). The longest gain for Cumberland was for a single ten-yard pass (on a 4th and 22!), and they accumulated a grand total of *negative* 42 rushing yards for the game!

WSB RADIO'S FIRST BROADCAST

1922

In early 1922 the United States was still in a state of transition from the end of World War I, with worries over the stark depression gripping Europe, and concerns about how much "normalcy" then-president Warren Harding had brought to the nation. The Lincoln Memorial was nearing completion and, in Atlanta, the Cyclorama Building had just been dedicated, housing the magnificent painting of the Battle of Atlanta paid for by former Union General John B. Logan. Atlanta's population had been booming since the turn of the century, now topping two hundred thousand, and the fight for women's political rights had just produced another local first—Mrs. Rebecca Latimer Felton was selected by Georgia governor Thomas Hardwick to fill the seat of recently deceased Senator Tom Watson. The first female U.S. senator, she was also the only female senator ever to serve from Georgia and the last former slave owner to sit in a national elective seat; she would serve just a single day. In another first, there was a new information medium present in Atlanta to broadcast her story, WSB Radio.

The early history of radio is shrouded in controversy and poor documentation. The earliest known experiments in wireless transmission are generally acknowledged to have been done by Michael Faraday in the early 1830s, with James Clerk Maxwell making other important contributions throughout the mid to late nineteenth century. These and other researchers' investigations culminated with Heinrich Rudolf Hertz, who demonstrated in the laboratory the validity of Maxwell's theories of electromagnetic transmission, proving that radio transmission was possible. Ironically, Hertz saw no potential use for this! Nikola Tesla, Alexander Popov, and Oliver Lodge all built and demonstrated crude wireless transmitting apparatuses in the late 1890s, but it was Guglielmo Marconi who obtained the first patent for a "radio device" in 1896, almost entirely based on the work of these other pioneers. Marconi, more a businessman than inventor, made no significant technical contributions to the field, but followed up his patent award by opening the first factory to build radio devices in 1899, in Chelmsford, England.

By the first decades of the twentieth century, commercial radio was still in its infancy, still very much in the realm of hobbyists. The Internet of its day, radio had a similar beginning and a similar meteoric rise in popularity, social acceptance, and eventual widespread use by the nation at large. The very first commercial broadcast station in the United States is usually identified as KDKA in Pittsburgh, Pennsylvania, but there are competing claims for KCBS in San Jose, California (1909), 9XM in Madison, Wisconsin (1914, 1916, or 1917, depending on the definition of "broadcast"), and WBL in Detroit, Michigan (1920). If government regulation can provide a standard, KDKA was indeed the first licensed commercial station, dating from October 27, 1920. Typical of the people involved in these stations, Frank Conrad, the chief engineer at KDKA, had been a "garage" hobbyist for years and began transmitting his own regular signals as early as 1916.

Early radio sets were generally homebuilt "crystal" sets, constructed from plans printed in early electronic hobbyist magazines, and later the *Atlanta Journal,* though the Electro Importing Company of New York City offered the first commercial kits as early as 1905. Electro advertised its kits as a great hobby for young men, as they "kept them at home" building instead of out getting into mischief with gangs and other unsavory activities. On the other hand, the *Atlanta Constitution* carried a story on July 27, 1909, claiming that a group of boys had set up a "burglar's club" in Los Angeles using the brand-new radio technology to coordinate their crimes and keep track of the police! The homebuilt "crystal" sets used an interesting natural phenomenon to capture radio transmissions. Operating without any power source other than the radio transmission itself, the sets employed a galena crystal as a semiconducting detector; a wire-wrapped coil as a tuner; a long wire strung outside as an antenna; and a pair of earphones for listening. The *Journal* became a big proponent of these simple, relatively easy-to-build systems, as the editorial staff had become convinced that radio was the wave of the future. In one February 1922 article, the paper claimed that "over 2,000" crystal sets were being used by hobbyists and enthusiasts in Atlanta alone.

There were several "ham operators" or amateur radio enthusiasts around Atlanta in the early 1920s, and several had approached Major John S. Cohen, the publisher of the *Journal,* with plans to bring the medium to the city. One of these early "radio-men," Walter Tison, a former Navy wireless operator, proved both persuasive and equipped to deliver. He offered Cohen the use of his own transmitter if he would hire him to set up and run a station for the paper. With the listening base in place and growing, the *Journal* decided to take up Tison's offer, and open its own radio station.

Operating with only 100 watts of power at 740 kilohertz, and only authorized to transmit weather reports at first, the *Journal's* WSB Radio began its broadcasting run on the evening of March 15. From a cramped room at the top level of their downtown building, the station broadcast a jazz rendition of "The Light Cavalry Overture." It was the 82nd licensed station and 27th commercial broadcast station to appear in the short, two-year span since KDKA had gone on the air. Although restricted to weather condition broadcasts, WSB also added farm reports, broadcasting twice a day for about an hour. The equipment of the time suffered from cooling problems and would suffer a catastrophic failure if left on for longer than that. Within a week, however, WSB started adding live music broadcasts, the first of which featured Fiddlin' John Carson, the seven-time "Champion Fiddler of Georgia." Carson was working as a housepainter in his nearby home neighborhood of Cabbagetown and reportedly walked up to the studio and told the new station manger, "Little Colonel" Lambdin Kay, he would "like to have a try at the newfangled contraption." Reportedly he was paid for the short bit of fiddling with a snort of the radio engineer's whisky, but this is unlikely. It was during Prohibition, after all, and radio engineers are noted for their serious, sober ways.

WSB proved a hit from the very beginning, leading the *Journal* to rapidly expand its operation and transmitting power. Expanded daytime broadcasts began by the fall of 1922, operations moved to the roof of the nearby Atlanta Biltmore Hotel in 1925, and the station joined the fledgling NBC network in 1927. An increase in broadcast power to 50,000 watts in 1933 and a move to the current 750 kilohertz broadcast frequency in 1935 allowed the station to be heard in the daytime all across the northern part of the state, with nighttime "skip" broadcasting heard across the country and regularly in several foreign nations. The *Journal's* long-time rival, the *Atlanta*

Constitution, opened its own radio station the same year, WGM, which got its license later but actually beat WSB on the air by a few days. The *Constitution* had worked with Georgia Tech's department of electrical engineering, which had its own experimental transmitter, and ended up turning over WGM's license and operation to Tech by the end of the decade. This station reopened in the 1930s as WGST, a CBS News affiliate.

Early radio programming was anything but consistent or highly cultured. Major Cohen said he was perfectly satisfied to have anyone who could do anything at all appear in his studio. As a result, "everyone in the community who could sing, whistle, play a musical instrument, talk, or even breathe heavily had performed for the invisible audience." More conventional programming quickly took over; WSB soon became and then remained the flagship station in Atlanta. By the late 1920s, all prominent visitors worth their salt made their way to its studios for appearances and interviews, and syndicated programs recorded in its studios aired all across the nation. The voice of the *Atlanta Journal* quickly grew into the voice of Atlanta and then became the "Voice of the South," helping usher the Gate City into the national spotlight as one of the cultural capitals of the country.

FRANK GORDY OPENS THE VARSITY

1928

Two short, seemingly rude sentences have come to epitomize one of Atlanta's culinary treasures: "Have your order on your mind and your money in your pocket," and the glad, usually shouted refrain "What'll ya have?" While many visitors to Atlanta expect to find marvels of Southern food traditions heralded and celebrated, to native Atlantans, the most celebrated restaurant in town features the lowly hot dog and battered onion rings. A whole lot of them, as well, at the world's largest drive-in restaurant, the Varsity.

In the early 1920s, Frank Gordy was an unwilling underclassman at the Georgia Institute of Technology in Atlanta, forced by his mother to attend the school and struggling in a losing battle to keep his grades up high enough to graduate with a degree in industrial management. Allegedly, one of his professors, unimpressed with his academic prowess, suggested that he drop out of school and open a hot dog stand instead. It was no doubt meant as an insult and Gordy denied the story later, but that is precisely what he did. Leaving Tech after less than a quarter of studies, Gordy finished his undergraduate degree at Oglethorpe College, then moved with his brother Herbert to Florida, hoping to cash in on the land boom that was still going on down there. The brothers ended up mostly going fishing, but Gordy noted the growing number of small, very popular "fast food" joints that were popping up all around the state. Gordy later recalled that instead of engineering principles, he had primarily been concerned with where he could find good, cheap food around the Tech campus and decided to set up such a place near his old school. His original plan was to build the restaurant, make it successful, then sell it for a nice profit. He achieved two out of these three goals.

Gordy's uncle, Bo Ingram, happened to own a building at the exact spot where the streetcar let off Tech students near the campus. This small, rundown building at the corner of Luckie Street and Hemphill Avenue, had a Texaco gas station, a small barbershop, and had formerly housed a small restaurant, the Yellow Jacket Inn. Frank thought it the perfect place to start and leased the space from his uncle in 1926, keeping the name of the former restaurant. It was not even a proper restaurant, described by one patron as "a little wooden shack with doors that raised up," but it was enough to house Gordy's chili pot, grill, and a small icebox that contained only Coca-Cola products, of course! The little hot dog shack was an immediate hit with Tech students. One later remarked that "most of us lived on Frank Gordy's hamburgers," and Gordy soon had to hire his first paid employee, then–high school student Epp Suddath. Suddath stayed with Gordy's restaurants for the next forty-three years.

Two years later, Gordy's stand was doing quite well, and he saw an opportunity to expand. Leasing an adjacent sixty-foot lot along North Avenue, Gordy closed the Yellow Jacket Inn, poured his total profits into a small, new, brick building and renamed his new restaurant the Varsity. The first night he was in business with his new place, Gordy took in $47.50 from more than three hundred customers, a tidy sum of money for the time and a very good omen for the future. Gordy's profits were very slim, his total food cost for a chili dog with onions and a napkin was four cents, and he sold them by the bushel-basket load for a nickel each, while plowing the profits back into building up his business.

The first drive-in restaurant was a small barbecue shack in Dallas, Texas, Kirby's Pig Stand, which opened in 1921, but the concept did not take off immediately. Gordy had never intended the Varsity to be a drive-in, but when the first car pulled up one day and honked its horn, one of his employees, Monk Suddath, Epp's brother, ran out to take the order. Gordy was not impressed, reportedly telling Monk, "If they want to eat, tell them to come inside." His reticence did not last long, however, as he saw the opportunity in exploiting the new car craze. He soon hired a few "curb boys" to take orders, and in 1936, expanded into another lot westward toward the Tech campus to provide a large parking lot.

"Carhops" as a cultural phenomenon came about in the 1930s, at the same time as the new car culture evolved in America. It is thought that the first carhops were employed by banks and drug stores, so their relatively wealthier customers would not have to make the arduous trek inside the buildings to do their business, but it did not take long for restaurants to adopt the concept. The name of these outdoor waiters and customer service staff came from another phenomenon of the time. Nearly every car had some form of running-board below its doors, and these were used by the mostly male waiters to "hop up" on, direct the car to a parking space, and take the orders. The name stuck but male dominance in the job did not, as these new "fast food" restaurant owners soon learned that pretty female faces on their carhops meant more business and larger orders.

Although the gender of carhops was overwhelmingly female at most fast food joints, it was not at the Varsity. Carhops there from the beginning were almost exclusively young, black men, who competed with each other to "hop" cars as they pulled into Gordy's expansive lot. John Wesley Raiford, aka "Flossie Mae," a veteran car-hop at the tender age of twenty, was one of Gordy's first hires for the expanded service. Like all the other carhops, he worked exclusively for tips and created his own unique look through his wild variety of hats, his "dance and sway," and his rapid-fire sing-song recitation of the menu, all to catch potential customers' attention. From 1937 to 1993 Raiford proved to be Gordy's most valuable selling point, bringing in as many customers as did the good food. His popularity was almost instantaneous; allegedly, Clark Gable heard of the unique carhop while in town for the premiere of *Gone with the Wind* in 1939 and asked to be taken to see him for supper one night. Raiford passed away in 1997.

Another of Gordy's famed employees was the late comedian Nipsey Russell, who honed his act on parking lot customers and spread the fame of the Varsity in his early television appearances. But Gordy's most effective hire was the late counterman Erby Walker. Walker was hired as a janitor at the age of fifteen in 1952, and although nearly fired the first night, stayed on working seven-day, one-hundred-hour weeks until just before his death in 2008. He eventually grew into a Varsity institution, ruling the order counter with the twin-coined catch phrases that have lived after him, shouted enthusiastically at each customer: "What'll ya have?" and when things got especially busy, "Have your money in your hand and your order on your mind!" Walker took an "early retirement" in 2003 to spend some more time with his grandchildren, but came back to work after just three weeks, unable to stay away from his second family at the Varsity.

Although there is little visual evidence to connect Georgia Tech and the restaurant in the downtown Varsity, it has a long and rich history linked directly to the adjoining Georgia Tech campus. Lunch there and home games at Bobby Dodd Stadium, a short stroll away, have long been traditional for both students and alumni, as are late-evening impromptu study sessions in one of the "television rooms." It is also a mecca for other sports fans and tourists who find their way to Atlanta, indulging in the Varsity's famous F.O.'s, onion rings, "glorified" burgers, and heavy dogs. One such football fan summed up Gordy's landmark restaurant best: "This is where fast food started, this is Atlanta."

Frank Gordy died on June 18, 1983, aged seventy-eight. The day of his funeral, June 21, was the first and only day the Varsity has closed since 1928.

THE PREMIERE OF
GONE WITH THE WIND

1939

Atlanta has never seen such an utterly and completely wild celebration as it did with the simple opening of a movie, before or since. The cold night of Friday, December 15, 1939, was the long-awaited event that everyone who was anyone scrambled to attend. As producers, stars, and various important persons exited their limousines in front of Loew's Grand Theater, a large throng of admirers and fans gathered in front cheering, shouting, and applauding lustily. The very last limousine arrived, carrying a short, almost plain-looking woman, who was helped out and escorted to a platform in front of the theater by none other than Mayor William B. Hartsfield himself. Margaret Mitchell, the author of the already famous novel the movie had been based on, waved to the crowd, and then went through the gaily decorated entrance to the great theater to the loud roar of the crowd. Once inside, she was escorted to her prominent seat among the great stars and politicians, but first paused to go and shake the hands of four old men sitting several rows behind. With that, she settled in to see her novel finally come to life on the big screen in *Gone With the Wind.*

One of the most popular novels ever written, it took Mitchell seven years to write, another eight months to edit and fact-check, and was the only novel she published in her lifetime. Her working title for the book was *Pansy,* the original name of her leading protagonist, and she based it largely on her experiences growing up in Atlanta at the knees, sometimes literally, of Civil War veterans, former slaves, and old-time socialites. There have been some suggestions made that Mitchell was also heavily influenced by two memoirs of the war, *Life in Dixie During the War* by Mary Gay, and the published diary of a South Carolina plantation owner's wife, Mary Chesnut. Mitchell had been incapacitated by a badly broken leg in 1911 and had voraciously read these and many other Civil War–era books during this time and again during recovery from a third leg injury in 1926. From the setting of the novel and her own family experiences, however, it is clear that she was not simply novelizing these two works.

Mitchell was born into a prominent and successful Atlanta family; her father Eugene was a lawyer and her mother, Mary Isabelle, called "Maybell" by nearly everyone, was a prominent suffragette. Margaret graduated from a top private prep school and was accepted to Smith College, but left in the middle of her freshman year to return home after her mother died unexpectedly in 1918, a victim of the influenza epidemic. Instead of settling down as the woman of the house, and then marrying into another prominent family to spend the rest of her life as a woman of leisure, as society dictated at the time, she defied the conventions and took a job as a cub reporter and later columnist for the *Atlanta Journal.* She did take the trouble to insist her informal name, Peggy, be used as her byline. She worked for the *Journal* as a regular reporter until 1926, bringing in a bit extra as a freelance columnist for the paper afterward, but by the fall of that year she was at work on what she at first thought would be a short story about life on a post–Civil War plantation.

As many other writers have also noted about their own experiences, she did not enjoy the literary life very much, later telling a friend that she "hated writing almost as much as Wagner and tap dancing," but persisted at the urging of her husband, John Marsh. The short story turned into a fifteen-thousand-word novella, *Ropa Caramagin,* which John dismissed as lacking in theme and as a poor example of the work he thought she could produce. Mitchell was discouraged, insecure about her talents as well as the life of writing, and put the work on hold for a few years, finding any excuse not to get back to work on it. Coming back to it in fits and starts, mostly at Marsh's urging, she reworked parts of it, renamed it *Pansy,* and wrote hundreds of more pages over the next eight years, mostly sitting at the living room window of their Atlanta home she not-so-fondly referred to as "the Dump." One particularity that dragged out her work was her obsessive attention to detail; she spent hours researching whether it had rained on a particular day of battle or which Confederate general was in the field at a particular time. Another reason for her lengthy and careful attention to her writing was her great fear of being sued if she wrote something negative that would be too closely identified with a living person, a legacy of her stiff and stern attorney father. She changed the time period to cover the range of antebellum life, wartime struggles around the middle Georgia plantation she had named Tara, and postwar life, mostly set in and around Atlanta.

In 1935 the vice president of the prominent publishing house, Macmillan Company, Harold Strong Latham, came to Atlanta in search of new writers and manuscripts. Tipped off by an acquaintance, he was introduced to Mitchell, who agreed to let him look at her unfinished work after several days of meetings and talks. Although her six-hundred-thousand-word treatment was incomplete and quite raw, to say the least, lacking a first chapter and consisting mostly of various envelopes containing chapters, rewrites, and revisions of different periods of time on the plantation, Latham was deeply impressed. Within two months of seeing the incomplete mess of Mitchell's work, he approved the project and offered her a contract with a $500 advance and healthy royalties. With the extensive help of her husband, and working through another series of illnesses and health problems, Mitchell was able to complete the novel by early February 1936. As submitted, it was still over four hundred thousand words long, far longer than the copy editors at Macmillan had been expecting. Mitchell, her husband John, editor Lois Cole, and principal copy editor Susan Prink painfully hammered out a final draft during the spring, and the book was finally published in June, with an initial run of ten thousand copies. Macmillan hoped to sell at least 27,500 copies total, but even before publication, indications were strong that it would be a blockbuster hit.

When Macmillan first announced its spring and summer list of publications in February 1936, immediate inquiries from several Hollywood studios came in about the new Civil War novel. One month after the book was published, producer David O. Selznick purchased the film rights for $50,000, a small fortune at the time, and a scandalous amount of money to be spent on what most producers thought a complete disaster of a premise at the box office. It is hard to say which was the harder prefilming task: condensing the novel to even a six-hour marathon of a movie or casting the major lead roles for what many nonproducers thought would be a blockbuster production. Screenwriter Sidney Howard's lengthy script was distilled to the four-hour production version by a host of uncredited writers, Clark Gable and Vivien Leigh were awarded the lead roles after a lengthy and turbulent selection process, and filming began in January 1939.

Production of the movie took an amazingly short amount of time for such a lengthy and complicated film, and December 15 was set as the premiere, to be held in Atlanta, of course. Loew's Grand Theater built a grandly elaborate columned façade for the occasion, completely ignoring the description of Tara given in the book, but closely replicating Selznick's equally inaccurate vision. Georgia Governor Eurith D. Rivers declared December 15 a state holiday, while Atlanta Mayor William Hartsfield went one further and declared the three-day schedule of events an official city festival, urging male residents to adopt Civil War–era sideburns and beards, and ladies to wear hoop skirts and pantalets for the occasion. After a nearly endless stream of press receptions, dances, parties, celebrity appearances (by even some actors not in the film, like Claudia Colbert), and a grand formal dress ball presented by the Atlanta Junior League, the whirlwind of excitement culminated in the premiere. The movie began shortly after Mitchell's arrival. There being relatively few seats in the theater, six thousand Atlantans filled the nearby City Auditorium, seeing and being seen, unable to get tickets to the premiere. Instead, they danced the night away at a lavish concert by the Kay Kyser Orchestra.

And who were the four men that Mitchell had paused to greet before the premiere? They were four honored and locally revered Confederate veterans who had fought in the very battle the film portrayed and had somehow lived another seventy-four years to see their great struggle played out on the big screen, in the premiere of *Gone With the Wind.* In the theater, these four, gray-uniformed and medal-bedecked veterans watched raptly as the sounds of bugle and battle stirred their ancient passions; J. A Skelton, ninety-two, James T. Pittman, ninety-two, J. R. Jones, ninety-five, and John

C. Dodgen, ninety-three, all reportedly appeared to relive a part of their youthful adventures as the mock battles unfolded on the screen. Dodgen had been a cavalryman, the very "cavalier" spoken of in the famous movie introduction, assigned to Co. B, the "Fulton Dragoons," Cobb's Legion, Cavalry Battalion, under Wade Hampton's Cavalry Brigade, Lee's Army of Northern Virginia. "General" Jones had been assigned to Co. A, the "Upson Sentinels" of the 46th Georgia Volunteer Infantry Regiment, Johnson's Army of Tennessee, had fought all through Georgia, Tennessee, and the Carolinas, and was present at the surrender in Durham Station. Skelton was a passenger on the train that the locomotive General was hauling, which was captured by Andrew's Raiders at Big Shanty; this episode was later heralded as the "great locomotive chase." He later served with the 7th Regiment, Georgia Infantry (State Guards), and as a guard at the notorious Andersonville prisoner of war camp. Pittman is believed to have served with Co. A, the "Thomasville Guards," 29th Georgia Volunteer Infantry Regiment, had fought in the Atlanta campaign, later in Tennessee, and surrendered in North Carolina.

THE BAND OF BROTHERS
MARCHES THROUGH ATLANTA

1943

In late November 1942, Colonel Robert F. Sink, commander of the 506th Parachute Infantry Regiment, sat at his desk in the training camp outside of Toccoa, Georgia, reading a *Reader's Digest* magazine article. In it, an American officer was expounding upon how advanced, tough, and capable the Japanese infantry were and used the example of how one Japanese battalion had covered one hundred miles of Malayan roads in just seventy-two hours. Sink had complete confidence that his new unit, having survived some of the hardest and most brutal training the Army has ever offered, could easily beat that record. He picked his hard-charging 2nd Battalion for the honor, which was led by Major Robert Strayer with his four companies of soon-to-be paratroopers: Dog, Easy, Fox, and Headquarters Companies. Easy Company was led by an already famous officer, First Lieutenant Herbert Sobel. One of his much more capable platoon leaders was a quiet man from Pennsylvania, Second Lieutenant Richard Winters, later famed for his war exploits in books and movies. At seven a.m. on December 1, 1942, Strayer led his battalion out of Camp Toccoa, heading toward Five Points in downtown Atlanta, 118 long, hard miles ahead.

Airborne Infantry, the use of parachute-equipped soldiers to drop highly trained but lightly armed and equipped units behind enemy lines, was a relatively new concept to the U.S. Army in 1943. Several nations had planned or experimented with airborne forces as early as World War I, but it was the German *Fallschirmjäger* (literally, "parachute hunters") that were first used in combat during the Danish and Norwegian campaigns of 1940. Massive German airborne operations shortly afterward during the campaigns for France and Crete convinced the United States that it needed to develop its own airborne forces. Ironically, the Crete operation was so costly in men and material, mostly due to heavily defended and rock-strewn drop zones, that the Germans never made another major drop. The first American paratrooper unit was formed in June 1940, a small Test Platoon at Ft. Benning, Georgia, that field-tested the first American combat parachute, the T-4, and developed a training program to build a large pool of trained paratroopers.

The first airborne combat unit was formed in September 1940, the 1st Parachute Battalion (soon reflagged as the 501st Parachute Battalion), while the United States was still technically at peace and neutral, a full year after World War II had started. The 502nd Parachute Battalion was formed in July 1941, but was still in the process of training when the United States entered the war in December. In 1942 the Army massively increased the number of airborne units, adding five full airborne divisions (the 11th, 13th, 17th, 82nd, and 101st), each with three Parachute Infantry Regiments, or PIRs, along with supporting artillery, signal, medical, and engineering units. Some of these units, especially those bringing in heavy equipment and supplies, used gliders instead of using parachutes. One of these units, the 506th PIR, was formed in July 1942 at the equally new remote Camp Toombs (later Camp Toccoa) in northeast Georgia.

The 506th PIR was placed under the command of Colonel Sink on its formation; he would be the sole American regimental commander to retain his command for the whole war. As one of the first airborne infantry officers, and as part of the original 501st Parachute Battalion, he was well aware of the extreme risks his men would take, dropped into the most dangerous areas to do some of the nastiest and heaviest fighting, all the time surrounded and away from any direct support from other units. To this end, he helped develop what would become one of the most difficult and demanding training courses in the Army, along with the "hardest obstacle course in the world," that each of his troopers would have to overcome on a daily basis. This training course would start with four months at Camp Toccoa, mostly for physical fitness and "weeding out" the unit, then several weeks at Ft. Benning near Columbus to learn parachuting skills and equipment, then several more weeks of advanced field training at Camp Mackall, North Carolina, near Ft. Bragg and Fayetteville. The training these Currahees endured is hard to imagine, even for most military veterans. A good hallmark is the numbers that they went through to get the final tally: Over 500 officers volunteered and began training, while only 148 made it through. Over 5,300 enlisted volunteers went through all or part of the grinding training regime, leaving 1,800 to fill the ranks before they entered combat!

All of these new airborne units chose battle cries and mottos that had American Indian connections, starting with the 501st's famous "Geronimo!" Paratroopers admired and felt a great kinship with the great Indian guerilla fighters of the nineteenth century, especially the Apache of the Southwest, who had never been defeated in battle throughout the Indian Wars period. Outside of Camp Toccoa was an isolated, steep-sided mountain called Currahee, named from the Cherokee word for "stands alone." The men of the 506th had an intimate familiarity with this mountain, forced to run the three miles from the camp to its peak and back again several times a week. As paratroopers were always going to be alone and isolated, they thought it an apt name, and adopted Currahee as the unit's motto.

In December 1942 the 506th was ready to move on to Ft. Benning. The 1st Battalion moved by train the entire way, while the 3rd Battalion took the train to Atlanta, marching from Terminal Station in downtown Atlanta 136 miles south to Ft. Benning. The 2nd, led by Major Strayer, moved out from the camp on the cold, rainy morning of December 1, marching at a quick pace toward Atlanta. Strayer was trying to help prove Sink's point, that American infantry was just as capable, if not more so, than anything the Japanese could put in the field, but he did not go about doing so the easy or most efficient way. Over 100 miles of the 118-mile route he chose was over unpaved, muddy roads, or through rough fields, with all the men carrying their full combat loads of personal equipment and weapons, including heavy machine guns and mortars. The first day's march started out in a heavy, cold fog, then changed to heavy rain and hail as they marched the forty miles to Gainesville. That night, as the men wrapped up in their shelter halves, still with their soaked uniforms on, the temperature dropped to below freezing. Wednesday morning, December 2, the men started out with still-frozen clothing, marching through half-frozen mud another forty miles to just outside of Buford, again bunking down on bare ground with only a thin shelter half for warmth.

The third day of rapid marching brought the Currahees to the campus of Oglethorpe University in DeKalb County. There, they had access to warm showers, a proper ground to pitch tents, and perhaps important to sagging morale due to the exertion and weather, groups of openly admiring reporters and tourists from

Atlanta. The last day's march was shorter, but was partially on paved roads, which proved harder on the paratroopers' feet than the soft, though heavy and clinging, mud they had been fighting through. With Atlanta civilians cheering them on, the men pulled themselves back into proper formations, forgot their aching feet and twisted ankles, and marched proudly into downtown by the afternoon of Thursday, December 3. As they turned down Peachtree Street to Five Points, a large crowd gathered on the sidewalks, bands played, Red Cross volunteers handed the muddy troopers packs of cigarettes, and motorcycle police escorted them to where Mayor Hartsfield was waiting, with a ribbon of the city's thanks and congratulations to attach to their colors. Assuming their ultimate destiny lay in the Pacific, Strayer accepted the ribbon, assuring the crowd that he and his men would "deliver it to Tokyo!"

It is sobering to look at the faces in the newspaper pictures of this march—heavily burdened, sopping wet young paratroopers happily mugging it up for the camera in the exhilaration of their youth. Many of them never came back home. One example is seen in the lead story about this march for the *Atlanta Journal*. Just under the headline, "Out-Marching The Japs," is a photo of a double column of Currahees marching down an Atlanta street, grinning ear to ear and waving at the photographer. In the front marches Private First Class (later Staff Sergeant) Roy H. Austin of Dog Company, an M-1 Garand slung over his shoulder, the poster-perfect image of a healthy American paratrooper. He parachuted into Normandy on June 5, 1944, fought there for five weeks, then parachuted in again near Eindhoven, Holland, fighting there for another seventy days, before being pulled out of the line just before the last German offensive of the war kicked off. He was killed in action during the successful assault and capture of Noville, Belgium, on January 15, 1945, near the end of the Battle of the Bulge.

THE DEADLIEST HOTEL FIRE

1946

It started with an elevator operator smelling smoke. In the end, it was the deadliest hotel fire in America. Ever. The hotel had been widely and consistently advertised as being fireproof. It turned out that it was, amazingly enough, but the people staying there on the night of December 7, 1946, weren't. On that day, the fifth anniversary of the Pearl Harbor attack, the Winecoff Hotel was filled to capacity, over 280 registered guests in 195 rooms of the fifteen-story brick building towering over Peachtree Street. By dawn the next morning, 119 of them were dead and another hundred seriously injured after a night of sheer terror.

William Fleming Winecoff had built his namesake hotel in 1913 at the corner of Peachtree and Ellis Streets, in the heart of downtown Atlanta. He turned over daily operations of the hotel just two years later to the Robert Meyer Hotels management firm, then sold the hotel in 1936 for a good profit to Ward Wight of the Tennessee Realty Company, but continued to live there with his wife in suites 1011 and 1012. The fifteen-story, 155-foot-high building cost Winecoff's firm a total of over $350,000 for construction and was worth an estimated $1 million in 1946, equal to roughly $10.8 million in current dollars. When it was built, it was classified as "fireproof": It had a steel, load-bearing frame, the steel girders wrapped in protective materials (probably asbestos) to protect them from weakening and losing their load-bearing potential in the event of fire; the floors and ceilings were concrete with tile fillers; the exterior walls were made of twelve-inch-thick brick; and the elevator shafts were tile-enclosed with well-protected wiring. It also featured an unprotected, open, central spiral staircase, which wrapped around the elevator enclosure leading from the lobby to the top floor.

Classifying construction as "fireproof" in the late nineteenth and early twentieth centuries was not a statement of safety; it was a reflection on the older type of construction common across the nation at that time. Most buildings were made of a brick shell, with small ledges to hold the ends of the unfastened wooden floor joists; the weight of the floor held them in place. In the event of fire, the wood and asphalt-shingled (or tar-papered) roofs would burn away fairly quickly, allowing hot gases and smoke to escape; then the wooden floors would burn and collapse into the basement without dragging the walls down with them. Afterward, all that was necessary was to clean out the basement and put up a new floor and a roof to get back into business quickly. The Winecoff's new style of construction was an architecturally progressive idea to make even that effort unnecessary, as the structure itself was unlikely to be damaged in any ordinary room or trash fire. Modern fire codes were not in effect at the time of its construction, so there were no sprinklers, exterior fire escapes, alarms, or fire doors for interior stairwells.

The Winecoff Hotel had its first brush with a serious fire on February 18, 1942. A single room fire in 1122 gutted the contents of just that one space and parts of the exterior hallway, but trapped dozens of guests in the upper floors due to the thick, choking smoke. Several people had to be treated for smoke inhalation, but no one was killed or seriously injured. The unlearned lesson, though, was that the "fireproof" hotel contained what firefighters call a "heavy fire load," which means furnishings, fixtures, and decorations that will burn inside the rooms and corridors, especially those that will easily ignite or produce toxic smoke. The Winecoff had been redecorated several times over the years, and in addition to the rooms filled with wooden furniture and horsehair-filled beds, some of the walls had as many as five layers of oil-based paints and wallpaper; some of these were covered with freshly painted burlap wall coverings called buckram, a fashion at the time. The painters were still at the hotel in early December 1946 and had stored several open and closed containers of paint and thinners in closets on several floors.

On the evening of December 6, the hotel hosted a number of returned war veterans and their families, who were still looking for proper housing in the postwar boomtown, a number of business travelers, some tourists, and a large number of teenagers who were in town for the annual Youth Assembly at the state capitol. A large and quite illegal poker game was going on as well, with a group of large, rough-looking men in room 330. Bell Captain Bill Mobley went to that room after midnight to ask the rowdy and drunken men to hold down the noise, just as bellhop Wayne Wise had done earlier in the evening. One of the gamblers, Roy McCullough, was a known felon and lifelong criminal with a vicious temper and violent nature, who had robbed a popular restaurant just a week earlier and was being sought by police that night. He had also served a prison sentence with Mobley some years earlier, and probably wasn't happy about Mobley's official visit.

A little after 3:30 a.m., elevator operator Rozena Neal was coming back down after taking some guests to the tenth floor, when she smelled smoke between the fourth and fifth floors. After alerting the night telephone operator, Catherine Rowan, she took her elevator back up to find Mobley, by then on an inspection of the upper floors, but stopped when she saw flames through the elevator window on the third floor. For some reason, Rowan did not immediately answer the telephone when Mobley called at about the same time, smelling smoke on the fifth floor. This delayed the first alert to the Atlanta Fire Department (AFD) by a few, critical minutes.

The AFD recorded the first call at 3:42 a.m. Four engines, three ladders, and a rescue unit responded to the scene within one minute, but when the first-in chief officer, Assistant Fire Chief F. J. Bowen, reported smoke showing from multiple floors on the Ellis Street side of the building, Chief of Department Charles C. Styron ordered a second and third alarm to be struck simultaneously, then a fourth alarm at 3:49 a.m. Arriving on the scene and quickly sizing up the overwhelming disaster developing in front of him, he ordered a "general alarm" struck at 4:02 a.m., bringing every available company and every off-duty fireman to the scene. As firemen and apparatus arrived and began setting up in the cramped streets and alleys around the hotel, they were already having to dodge suitcases flung out of upper-floor windows by trapped guests trying to get their attention. Within a few more minutes, as the fire raced through the building, they were also dodging falling bodies.

With the general alarm call came an automatic call for mutual aid from all the surrounding city and county fire departments. All told, forty-nine pieces of apparatus responded, including eleven ladder and thirty-two engine companies. Ladder 1, the largest ladder truck the AFD possessed, an American LaFrance one-hundred-foot wooden "stick," was out of service that night, as well as one of the two eighty-five-foot aerials, but the remaining ladder trucks used their fifty-five- through eighty-five-foot sticks to begin rescuing guests already standing at the window ledges of their rooms, as well as deploying every one of their remaining ground ladders to reach guests on lower floors. The biggest problem was that the highest of these ladders could barely reach the eighth floor of the fifteen-story building. Guests in upper-story rooms began putting together bed-sheet ropes to try and lower themselves to the point where firefighters could reach them; a few of these attempts were actually successful. As fires explosively breached the doors of upper-floor rooms, many guests not yet overcome from the smoke and gases could not hold on any longer and jumped from their windows.

While the laddermen were conducting external rescues, engine crews were pushing attack lines up the spiral staircase, taking a beating from the intensely hot, rapidly spreading flames. Due to the concrete construction of the hotel, the flames consuming the wall treatments, carpets, and furnishings grew extremely hot, heating the building up like an enclosed oven. Light fixtures and some exposed metalwork actually melted in the inferno, a sign the fire had reached temperatures of at least 1,200 degrees in some spots. This was in the days before modern "bunker suits," adequate helmets, and air packs came into service, and the firefighters leading the interior attack were continually overcome by the heat and smoke, requiring fresh crews to rush in, bring them out, and man the lines again. It took until 6:30 a.m. for the firefighters to reach the fifteenth floor, fighting extensive fire on every floor on the way up. Chief Bowen had led the first interior attack, but was overcome and hospitalized, as were two other officers who suffered heart attacks during the attack; several others were overcome by smoke. Fireman A. J. Burnham of Ladder 7 was the most seriously injured firefighter on the scene: A falling body struck him and knocked him off his ladder as he was performing a rescue. He survived but with serious back and other injuries.

One hundred nineteen people died in the fire, forty-one due to burns, thirty-two due to suffocation, twenty-six due to traumatic injuries from falls; the rest of the bodies were too badly damaged to determine a definitive cause of death. The largest amount of fire damage was found on the eighth through the tenth floor, but bodies were found on every floor except the first and second. Although no one was ever officially charged with setting the fire, and the fire was never formally ruled as intentionally set, several authors have laid down a clear case that McCullough, a lifelong habitual criminal, had set the Winecoff fire in order to take revenge on someone in the hotel, probably Mobley. Known as the "Candy Kid" after robbing an Atlanta candy factory as a teenager, he was also accused of setting a fire in the Ben Hill prison camp a few years earlier for the same reason. McCullough was arrested for the earlier restaurant robbery the same day of the fire and never left prison for the rest of his life, dying in 1964. He was buried in the prison yard a week later, after his body lay unclaimed and unvisited.

THE TEMPLE BOMBING

1958

In the late 1950s, Atlanta stood at a unique and dangerous crossroads of social and political change. The last Confederate soldiers had only recently died, and memorials and monuments to the Lost Cause abounded all around the city. White supremacist groups like the resurgent Ku Klux Klan still wielded some power, having regained political prominence in the 1920s, still openly walked the streets in broad daylight (occasionally), and acted on occasion as if they still ruled things as they had in the 1930s and 1940s. Opposed to these entrenched attitudes was the active civil rights movement, building in influence and power and directly countering and challenging the Old South status quo in nearly every aspect. Finally, business and cultural elites of the city, attempting to shed the old, segregationist, and secessionist labels, had turned Atlanta into an international mecca of the New South. All of these forces collided in the early morning hours of October 12, 1958, in a single act of terror that harmed no one directly, but which helped to change the culture of Atlanta for good.

It all started with an anonymous phone call to the United Press International office in Atlanta at two a.m. The caller warned that a bombing would take place that night, but with no further details, the warning was shrugged off as just another hoax. At 3:37 a.m. a bomb thought to be composed of forty to fifty sticks of dynamite exploded in a recessed side entrance on the northwest wall of the Hebrew Benevolent Congregation Temple, better known simply as the Temple, the oldest synagogue in Atlanta. The blast was loud enough to rattle the city and break windows in nearby buildings, but as the Temple sits on a low hill, and the blast took out a wall away from the street and did not start a fire, police dispatched to the area were initially unable to find anything. At 3:45 a.m. the UPI office received a second phone call, presumably from the same person. "General Gordon of the Confederate Underground," announced the caller. "We bombed a temple in Atlanta. This is the last empty building in Atlanta we will bomb." The caller went on to threaten all businesses that were owned by or employed blacks or Jews, saying, "Negroes and Jews are hereby declared aliens."

The reaction to the bombing by Atlanta's political and business elite was swift and absolutely condemning. The Temple was attended by the elite and wealthy Reform Jewish community in town, led by a popular Pittsburgh native and World War II veteran rabbi, Jacob M. Rothschild. He arrived soon after being alerted of the bombing by the building maintenance man, who was the first to discover the crime shortly after he arrived for work at 7:30 a.m. Rothschild was shocked at the extent of the damage, but not entirely surprised by the action; since coming to Atlanta, he had become an increasingly strident voice in support of civil rights. Mayor William B. Hartsfield arrived on the scene early on, absolutely and resolutely condemning the bombing, offering a thousand-dollar reward on the spot for information about the guilty party. While sifting through the wreckage with Rothschild, he ordered his police chief, Herbert Jenkins, to use every resource at his disposal to find out who had done it.

Jenkins did not need a platoon of detectives to figure out what general group he was looking for or what their motivations were. "The Confederate Underground" was not actually a formally organized group, but a well-known cover name for ad hoc terrorist activities by Klansmen. "General Gordon" was a long-dead but still well-respected Confederate general from Atlanta, who would have been appalled at being linked to these criminals. Since the lynching of Leo Frank in 1913, a resurgent Ku Klux Klan had come into great political and social power, not just in Georgia or the South, but all across the nation. At one point in the 1920s, the center of Klan power was in Indiana, with open membership common across the Midwest and Northeast. In the South, however, the Klan's power reigned nearly supreme. By the late 1920s, it was almost impossible to get elected to political office in any of the states of the Deep South without either membership in or the direct support of the Klan. The Klan saw itself as the protector of pure white Southern traditions, much like Hitler's SS saw itself as protecting an equally mythical Aryan bloodline, and it violently reacted against those thought to be lazy, abusive to their women, or users of alcohol (more so than the Klan members themselves, that is). It also enforced legal prohibitions against the races mixing in public or private settings.

During the prewar years, the Klan's activities were primarily directed against the black population, with Roman Catholics and foreigners in general also feeling their wrath. Many prominent Klansmen saw great kinship in the rise of the National Socialists in Germany under Hitler after 1932, agreeing heartily with them that Jews were the source of most, if not all the problems of the world. Outside of the South, Klan membership declined a bit during the late 1930s, but in the upper Midwest, a practically identical ideology sprang up in the form of American Nazi and German-American Bund parties. With World War II winding down in 1945, revelations of the mass murder of the Holocaust caused most of these anti-Jewish groups to disappear, at least openly. In the South, though, the Klan took up the cause of anti-Semitism, aided by several Democratic splinter parties that openly agitated against "communist Jews" and promoted some of the same ideas about unlikely Jewish conspiracies that Hitler's propaganda ministers had either made up or resurrected from equally unlikely medieval sources.

The Temple was not the first synagogue to be targeted by these domestic terrorists or even the only one to be attacked that same week. Anshel Emeth Temple in Peoria, Illinois, was bombed two nights later; both of these bombings followed similar attacks on synagogues in Miami, Florida; Charlotte and Gastonia, North Carolina; Nashville, Tennessee; Jacksonville, Florida; and Birmingham, Alabama. A federal and state task force had already been established by October 1958 in response to the earlier attacks, and reaction to the Atlanta crime was swift. Five men from one of the small political splinter groups, the nascent National States Rights Party (NSRP), were indicted on October 17 by the Fulton County grand jury in Atlanta. Named in the indictment were Wallace Allen, Robert Bowling, George Bright, Luther Corley, and Chester Griffin. All of these men were well-known violent members of the anti–civil rights movement; in fact Griffin was immediately linked to the bombing and picked up by Atlanta Police Department detectives the very next night. All five had the means, opportunity, and most definitely the motive to carry out this and other bombings.

Led by the notorious and violent segregationist, Jesse Benjamin "J. B." Stoner, the NSRP was formed in August 1958 in Jeffersonville, Indiana, from the remnants of several other earlier groups, including Stoner's own Christian Anti-Jewish Party and United White Party. Stoner, a lawyer by trade, was investigated by the FBI for a series of bombings of black churches in Alabama during the 1950s and 1960s, but was not indicted at the time for those crimes; he was convicted in 1980 and served time for a separate 1958 church bombing. A perpetual candidate for political office later in life, he was perhaps not successful because of his wildly non-mainstream political position; he ran one campaign as the "candidate of love," but during the same campaign slung racist epithets around like talismans and claimed Hitler was "too moderate" when it came to the Jews. He also stated that black people were not really human but were extensions of the ape family and Jews were "vipers from hell." All of his views were promoted in an in-your-face manner in television commercials he had sued successfully in federal court to have aired. He was, at least, consistent with these views; in a 1946 interview with an Atlanta newspaper, he stated that "being a Jew (should) be a crime punishable by death."

Griffin, the first of the conspirators to be arrested, was also the "weak link" of the group and the one most likely to spill the story. He did so, and fast, in great detail, while sitting on a children's swing set in Grant Park. He was, according to the detectives, paranoid that hidden microphones might record his initial verbal confession and find its way back to his Klan buddies. He said that Bright was the one who had set up everything and built the bomb with a lot of input and coaching from Stoner, who had supplied the dynamite. His later long and detailed written confession laid out exactly what each member of the group had done, including details such as their arguments over the color of the car they would use and what type of suitcase the bomb would be packed in. He also gave the details of where every member of the group had been stationed that night and stated that Stoner had left on a "business trip" earlier in the day, so he could claim some separation from the actions he had assisted.

The trials began with *State v. George Bright,* on December 1, 1958, in Fulton County Superior Court under Judge Durwood T. Pye. Bright's attorney, James R. "Jimmy" Venable, was the former mayor of Stone Mountain, came from the very family that once owned Stone Mountain itself, and not coincidentally, was the Imperial Wizard of the National Knights of the Ku Klux Klan. His usual courtroom tactic in such cases was soon in full display, subpoenaing every organization that had any possible relationship to the case for lists of "Jewish-born" members, employees, contributors, or subscribers, including both of the major Atlanta newspapers and WAGA-TV, and trying with a heavy-handed flurry of legal motions to change the trial into a general indictment of Jews. Pye was not the sort to engage in these shenanigans and soon had what to all appearances was a fair and full trial underway. However, despite Griffin's testimony and that of an undercover FBI informant in on the plans, as well as physical evidence found in Bright's residence, the jury eventually deadlocked at 9 to 3 in favor of a conviction, resulting in a mistrial. Bright was tried again in January 1959; this time, the jury acquitted him, and the Fulton County solicitor reluctantly dropped the charges against the remaining conspirators.

The end result was that no one was ever held criminally responsible for the bombing. It did, however, have the effect of bringing about a much harsher public condemnation of such terrorist actions, as well as helping to create a more favorable environment for civil rights progress and the peaceful actions of civil rights activists. The FBI's director, J. Edgar Hoover, had already been investigating the Klan and other violent anti–civil rights groups; this case spurred him to increase his department's infiltration and investigation of these groups. It also helped bring about greater public awareness of Jews in American society, set against the twin backdrops of ancient homegrown hatred and Hitler's maddened Holocaust. Stoner, though, remained unrepentant to the end. In a 2004 interview with the *Atlanta Journal-Constitution,* he described himself as a "soldier of Christ," adding that with his impending death, "I guess God will put his hand on my head and bless me." He died on April 23, 2005, at a largely African-American-staffed nursing home in northwest Georgia.

LENOX SQUARE MALL OPENS

1959

The 1950s was a time of rapid growth for Atlanta, but an even more rapid period of growth for what had become known as "metropolitan Atlanta," the immediate surrounding counties that were not included in the city limits proper. In 1900 Atlanta was listed as the fortieth largest city in America, but by 1950 it was the twenty-third largest city, due in part to the wild spurt of growth just before and during World War II. This growth, however, soon tapered off inside the city limits, leading to population loss for an extended period of time, but the surrounding metropolitan area kept on growing at accelerated rates. The primary reasons for this outer-area growth were the improvement of roads, including the first interstate highways begun in the mid-1950s; the wider availability of automobiles, even for those with smaller incomes; and a general desire for more "elbow room" and quieter surroundings in the suburbs. One after-effect of this move outside of the central city was the corresponding need for goods and services in the new suburbs, which led in turn to the opening of the first true shopping mall in the Southeast, Lenox Square.

It wasn't until well after the Civil War ended that Atlanta started seriously growing and expanding; the northern limit of any city infrastructure for a protracted time was the aptly named North Avenue. Around 1900, some of the wealthier Atlanta families started building grand homes well north of North, along an extended Peachtree Street into Buckhead. This suburban community was named after a large deer's head mounted outside of Henry Irby's general store and tavern, built in 1837 at what is today the intersection of West Paces Ferry and Roswell Roads. Just outside the main Buckhead settlement was a seventy-four-acre cotton and corn farm owned by John Simpkins, who witnessed but escaped the destructive wrath Union General William Sherman brought to the area in 1864. The major reason Buckhead was spared was that no rail line connected the community to Atlanta; the prominent Norfolk Southern rail line that runs through Buckhead today was built after the Civil War in 1873.

Simpkins lived until 1926, but sold his farm and property to First National Bank of Atlanta president John Ottley in 1897. Like many wealthy Atlantans, Ottley wanted to build a summer home (eventually called Joyeuse) to escape the noise and pollution of the city, and this property was easily accessible by the new Southern Railway line running across the eastern edge of his fields. As an acknowledgment of Ottley's wealth and status, the Southern railroad made his property a special stop for his convenience, and he built his own private station for that purpose. This station sat where the modern MARTA-Lenox transit line station was built in the 1980s. Ottley's twelve-room, beautifully decorated home soon became a favored place for the many parties and balls he and his wife threw during the hot summers, but living in such high-profile ways in such a remote area had its pitfalls. On July 6, 1933, a pair of somewhat incompetent criminals kidnapped Ottley from the driveway of his home, sending a note back to his Atlanta business demanding a ransom of $40,000, but releasing him unharmed before the note had even been delivered.

Ottley lived at Joyeuse until his death in 1945. The property was soon sold and made into apartments and small businesses, housing the many wartime veterans moving into the area. On May 22, 1956, the property was resold, this time to the developer Ed Noble, who immediately began clearing and grading the land, with plans to build a massive shopping center there. Ottley's home had been built on top of a low granite hill that rose above a dirt road on the north side, later paved and renamed Lenox Road, and was fronted on the west side by narrow, unpaved Peachtree Street. Noble's development company dynamited the hill away completely, leveling the entire property and lowering it all below the level of the adjacent roads.

Lenox Square Shopping Center, designed by architect Joe Amisano of the Toombs, Amisano, and Wells architectural firm, was completed by the summer of 1958, but did not have its grand opening until August 3, 1959. It was, in its original incarnation, an eight-hundred-thousand-square-foot, multilevel open-air center, with two large "anchoring" stores, fifty other shops, and a bowling alley and indoor golf range. It was by far the largest retail business in Georgia and most other Southern states. With its expansive parking lots (with "acres of free parking," according to early advertisements), it was one of the largest single entities in Georgia, larger and more populous by day than many small cities and towns across the state. It had been planned from the start to be one of the first "regional" shopping centers, attracting customers from not only the immediate community but also from across Georgia and neighboring states.

Despite warnings that it was a poor business decision, and that the new center was bound to fail (as "no-one lived out there," according to one local expert), Richard Rich decided to open his first suburban store at Lenox Square, soon followed by a second one at Decatur's newly built Belvedere Plaza Shopping Center, opening the same year. Rich's was joined at Lenox Square by its archrival Davison's department store, the two anchoring dead opposite ends of the sprawling center. Colonial Stores, then one of the region's biggest grocery store chains, built its largest store on the eastern end of the center, with a staggering (for the time) 31,500 square feet of Southern food goodness and the last word in glistening displays, counters, and checkout lines.

When it opened, Lenox Square was not much like the typical mall of today; it was more like an extended and multilevel strip mall, with an open center court decorated by flying concrete buttress-styled arches over grassy areas flanked by concrete benches and several small collections of sculptures depicting Southern folktales. The center was deliberately larger than what the relatively short list of tenants would need; several shops, including a Detroit-based Kresge Five and Dime Store (later K-Mart), were built on two levels, connected by stairwells or escalators. With great patronage and support from businesses in the first years, Lenox almost immediately started expanding the complex, adding more stores in a lower-level stretch along the eastern flank of the property and a movie theater that opened in June 1963. Lenox started a definite trend in shopping patterns; downtown Atlanta businesses experienced a downward trend that has not yet fully abated, fueled by other shopping centers and seven true malls opening all around the perimeter of the city over the next ten years.

With great pressure coming from the new and customer-preferred, enclosed, air-conditioned malls, Lenox underwent a major remodeling in 1971 and 1972. The second level was enclosed and air-conditioned and a third wing added, which housed what is still the only Neiman Marcus store in Georgia. Eight years later, another major expansion removed the bowling alley (the golf range disappeared sometime in the 1960s); the open courtyard in front of Davison's (and the sculptures there) with its adjacent Civil Defense bomb shelter; as well as the Colonial grocery store and its adjacent shops. A three-story atrium with surrounding multilevel retail spaces, a food court, an office tower, and an adjacent hotel were added; the large and well-attended theater was remodeled into an awkward and unbeloved multiplex, and two more large parking decks were added. Four years later, in 1980, a MARTA rapid transit rail station opened just outside the new expansion, radically increasing the customer base. Expansion projects in 1995 and 2007 added a third level and expanded some operating stores, giving Lenox a total of some 1,545,000 square feet of retail space in 240 stores, now the second largest retail mall in Georgia. (The Mall of Georgia in nearby Gwinnett County with 1.7 million square feet of retail space opened in 1999.)

There had been a great deal of negative press about the new shopping center when it first opened. Businesses inside worried that it truly was in an economic wasteland, while downtown business owners worried that it wasn't. It turned out not only to be a fiscal and community success but it also changed the entire face of the retail industry in Georgia. Before Lenox, shopping for anything more than immediate necessities was done downtown, primarily at large, flagship department stores scattered around the central business district. Lenox helped redirect the retail movement in Atlanta to local strip shopping centers backed by large regional shopping malls, with the downtown area relegated primarily to government services, nonretail business, arts, sports, and cultural events.

The move to shopping centers also marked the beginning of the end for locally owned, operated, revered, and loyally patronized large department stores. Richard Rich died in 1975, and his heirs sold the chain to Federated Department Stores the following year. The other local store, Davison's (originally Davison-Paxon-Stokes), had sold out to New York–based Macy's in 1925, which kept the local name until 1986. In 1994, Federated purchased all the holdings of R. H. Macy and Company, changing the name of the long-beloved local institution first to Macy's-Rich's, then dropping founder Morris Rich's name altogether on March 6, 2005.

MARTIN LUTHER KING JR.'S FUNERAL

1968

It was the nearest thing to a full-blown national state funeral that Atlanta has ever hosted, but not one that every citizen sought to attend. An Atlanta-born, internationally recognized and lauded man had been taken in the prime of his life, gunned down by a lone assassin, presumably, while at the pinnacle of his power and influence. But in his own hometown, this man had been branded a Communist-influenced agitator and troublemaker by none other than the state governor himself, his passing ultimately celebrated in certain communities. On the morning of April 9, 1968, Rev. Martin Luther King Jr.'s body lay in a mule-drawn wagon, slowly moving past hundreds of thousands of mourners lining the streets of downtown Atlanta. As the slow procession wound past the state capitol building, Georgia Governor Lester Maddox sat at his desk inside, officially ignoring the funeral, protected in his fear of what was going on by sixty-four helmeted state troopers clad for riot-control and 160 Georgia National Guardsmen.

King was born on January 15, 1929, in Atlanta, on the eastern edge of the "colored" business district along Auburn Avenue, which had been segregated as a result of the 1906 race riots. A bright scholar, he graduated from Morehouse College with a degree in sociology at age nineteen and became an associate pastor at his father's Ebenezer Baptist Church, a few blocks west of his boyhood home on Auburn that same year. After graduating from Crozer Theological Seminary in Chester, Pennsylvania, with a Masters of Divinity degree, he was ordained in the Baptist church and called to the pulpit of the Dexter Street Baptist Church in Montgomery, Alabama, in 1954. The following year, Rosa Parks refused to give up her seat in the "colored" section of a Montgomery city bus to a white man. Her arrest spurred King to put his sermonizing calls for racial equality to action in the political cause of civil rights.

King's entire career as a civil rights activist lasted just thirteen years. His early and consistent calls for nonviolent protest against Jim Crow laws and traditions were readily accepted at first, but by the mid-1960s were being challenged by more violent calls to action by rival civil rights figures. In March 1968, he had accepted a request from the sanitation workers of Memphis, Tennessee, to help them in securing a new contract guaranteeing them more equitable work conditions and recognition for their union from the city. King first arrived on March 18 to speak at a mass rally, and then returned on March 28 to lead what was supposed to be another peaceful march through the middle of the city. Instead, just seven blocks and twenty-five minutes after the march started, a violent riot broke out. King was driven out of the chaotic frenzy without injury, but one sixteen-year-old accused looter was killed, over sixty others were transported to hospitals for treatment of injuries, and 280 were arrested. King, demoralized and feeling his influence slipping away in the swirling violence around his hotel, spent the rest of the night fielding phone calls and watching the televised reports of the riot. King confided to his two ever-present associates, Ralph Abernathy and Bernard Lee, "Maybe we just have to admit that the day of violence is here, and maybe we just have to give up and let violence take its course."

King returned to Memphis on April 3, checking into his usual room 306 at the Lorraine Motel shortly after arriving. It was on the balcony outside that room the following evening that he was shot in the throat, directly through the knot of his necktie, by a single shot fired presumably from an awkward and unusual sniper's position in a flophouse seventy yards away. The perpetrator of this act was allegedly a small-time criminal and escaped convict named James Earl Ray. King was pronounced dead an hour later. Within hours of the initial newsflash, in some cases even before the final confirmation of King's death, riots broke out in dozens of cities across the nation.

One prominent Atlantan who felt the pain of King's assassination most personally was Mayor Ivan Allen, Jr. He and King had become close friends after meeting at a dinner to honor King's Nobel Prize in 1965. When he saw the televised news flash, he immediately called Coretta King to see if there was anything he could do to help. There was, as King was not yet deceased, and Allen and his wife rushed Mrs. King to the airport to catch the first plane to Memphis. The news of King's death reached them just before she boarded the flight. With no need to rush any longer or to get to Memphis, Allen escorted Mrs. King back home and sat with her in dazed silence. When Allen returned later in the evening to his city hall office, he received a call from Robert Woodruff, the former president and powerfully influential board member of Coca-Cola, offering to financially take care of anything the city might need in the coming days, a literal blank check offered to make sure the arrangements and funeral for King would go off without a hitch.

On the other hand, Governor Maddox, one of the last of the old breed of obstructionist, "stand in the doorway," segregationist Southern governors, was convinced that King had been a threat to the nation and refused to allow his body to lie in state inside the capitol rotunda. He also initially refused to order state flags to be flown at half-mast, finally talked into issuing the order by Secretary of State Ben Fortson, who pointed out that President Johnson had directed this to be done in public buildings across the nation. Maddox also announced that the day of King's funeral would be a regular workday, an order that was widely ignored for a number of reasons by state employees.

Large crowds had been expected for the funeral, but far more turned up than even the most extreme estimates; somewhere in the neighborhood of thirty thousand people crowded the small space in front of Ebenezer Baptist Church on Auburn Avenue. Crowds of celebrities showed up, including Vice President Hubert Humphrey and then-presidential candidate Richard Nixon; Jacqueline Kennedy and members of her family; numerous prominent national politicians; sports and entertainment figures; and various people in the spotlight; but to those of King's inner circle, the problem was, ironically, the race of so many of them. Ralph Abernathy would later write in his memoir that he recognized something was wrong while he stood at the front door of the crowded church. "I realized: This is Ebenezer Church, yet most of the people jamming the pews were white."

Eventually, over one thousand people crowded into the hot and humid sanctuary that normally could hold a maximum of 750. Following opening prayers, tributes, and hymns, King himself gave his own funeral sermon. A recording of one of his last appearances at Ebenezer was played, King's voice resonating through the crowded sanctuary with his "Drum Major Instinct" sermon. It began, "Every now and then I think about my own death, and I think about my own funeral. And I don't think of it in a morbid sense. Every now and then I ask myself, 'What is it that I would want said?'" Watching King's young children reacting to his voice, looking eagerly up at the empty pulpit for him, even hardened civil rights workers and usually stoic reporters and photographers wept openly. Afterward his coffin was carried out to a mule-drawn, hastily obtained old farm wagon, the thick crowd slowly parting to give way for the procession to Morehouse College and a final eulogy and celebration of King's life.

The four-mile route from the church was lined with an estimated quarter-million people, a "frighteningly enormous" crowd according to King's lieutenant Andrew Young, with at least another ten thousand people marching behind King's humble wagon. Even with such a massive crowd, it was almost completely silent; many people later remarked that about all you could hear was the steady clip-clop of the mules slowly pulling the wagon through the streets of Atlanta. An estimated 120 million people followed the procession on television, roughly half the nation's population at the time. Atlanta was closed for business for the day, nearly every shop shuttered, with every resident either on the street or sequestering themselves at home. Rich's Department Store, where King had been arrested some years earlier for attempting to integrate the old-South traditional lunchroom, had placed a large floral wreath in tribute to him on their closed front doors. The same types of tributes spontaneously occurred across the nation, the still-smoldering riots in multiple cities ending for the day, most not to be resumed afterward.

As the progression rounded Capital Avenue and passed directly next to the state capitol building lined with heavily armed state troopers and Guardsmen, King's old Southern Christian Leadership Conference (SCLC) compatriots escorting the wagon began singing softly "We Shall Overcome," an equally quiet rebuke to the sequestered governor peeking out at the proceedings from behind his shuttered windows.

The Old South had already changed, part for the worse, part for the better, but Old Atlanta showed its best side for its fallen son. With the single prominent exception of the governor, white citizens who had politically opposed King and hate-filled bigots of all stripes and races kept their peace, following the ancient Southern tradition of respectful consideration for the dead and mourning. Remarkably, though there were riots large and small in 126 other American cities in the days leading up to the funeral, with at least forty-six deaths as a result, not one single violent incident marred Atlanta during the days of King's memorial.

Martin Luther King Jr.'s funeral was remarkable for one other thing; it came on the day of the 103rd anniversary of Confederate General Robert E. Lee's surrender of his army to Union General Ulysses S. Grant, effectively ending the Civil War. So many years after the war that put an end to the practice of slavery, a black man murdered by a white man rode in honored tribute through the Gate City in the heart of the old Confederacy, while the powerful white segregationist governor of the fifth state to secede from the union hid in his office behind a phalanx of heavily armed guards. The symbolism of the changing face of the South was impossible to miss.

ICE STORM

1973

People who move to Atlanta from places that have serious snowfall several months of the year usually find great humor in the way this city handles its winter weather. There is usually a week or more of sober-faced television meteorologists giving dire warnings about the situation, complete with "Snow Jam (fill in year)" graphics; bread and milk disappear from grocery-store shelves within hours of the first forecast; the news reports fill up with long lists of school, business, and church closings well before anything actually happens; and if the winter weather event actually does happen, it is usually at most an inch or less of snow and some ice on the streets. This is a very real social and cultural event, usually occurring around the middle of January, which is amusing to most people outside of the city or state, but which is taken very seriously by long-term Atlanta residents for two reasons: the peculiarities of Atlanta weather and a single winter storm that started on January 7, 1973.

Atlanta's winter weather is not typical of what one might expect of a state in the Deep South; the Appalachian Mountains north of the city act as a funnel to channel cold air from the northeast during the winter months, setting up what is locally called the "wedge effect" of cold, humid air, and lots of fog around most of the metro area, while the Gulf of Mexico south of the city provides plenty of moisture to mix with the cool air aloft, even when the ground temperature is well above freezing. Most of the time, this results in a light snowfall with nothing sticking to the ground for more than a few hours. The city itself does not usually get much in the way of snowfall, less than two-and-a-half inches annually, but there have been some significant exceptions. Five inches fell on January 18, 1992, as part of a true blizzard that swept across the northern arc of the state that day; four inches fell on February 18, 1979; and just under eight inches of snow fell on March 24, 1983, the record for a single-day's snowfall in Atlanta.

Snow is usually not a problem, as most any Northern driver could tell you; it is ice that causes cars to lose traction and results in carnage on the roads. Certain weather phenomena combine to create the worst scenarios. A powerful low-pressure system in the Gulf of Mexico pumps in warm tropical moisture riding up over a cooler surface layer created by an equally strong high-pressure system further north, setting up an enhanced wedge effect that brings the surface temperature down to just at or slightly below freezing. The resulting precipitation begins as a cold rain or rain mixed with sleet and soon turns into solid ice on any surface it touches. Most of the worst events begin just after noon with the temperature rising just above freezing about mid-afternoon, and then falling as the afternoon goes on. As more precipitation falls, it partially melts the icy surfaces and then refreezes thicker, heavier, and harder as the temperature continues to drop below thirty-two degrees, resulting in what is called an "ice storm." The immediate danger for anyone caught out away from home is that the streets rapidly develop a glaze of ice with a very thin water topping, one of the slipperiest surfaces imaginable, and one that is nearly impossible to walk or drive over. The secondary issue is that the heavy ice coating soon starts to cause power lines, tree limbs, and even whole trees to collapse from the weight, tearing down telephone poles and remaining power lines; cutting off electricity and phone service to homes and businesses; further blocking accessible streets; and damaging the roofs and walls of structures.

Most forecasters did not foresee the dangerous aspects of the January 1973 storm as it was developing, predicting that it would rain lightly to moderately on the afternoon of January 7, cease, and then the temperature would drop below freezing for the next day or two. Most expected whatever moisture was still on the streets and trees to be dried up by the previously prevailing low humidity before it was frozen by the falling temperatures. The precipitation total for that day ended up far higher than forecast, a record 3.48 inches, but it did not come down as just cold rain as forecast. Instead, it first came down as sleet around noontime and then changed into the worst possible form, freezing rain, as the afternoon progressed. It did not snow at all that day, but by nightfall there was as much as two inches of ice covering some areas of the metro area as the temperature rapidly dropped below freezing, and the freezing rain continued throughout most of the night. For the next ninety-six hours the temperature did not rise above 32 degrees.

Atlanta is still a heavily forested city but was much more so in the early 1970s before the era of bigger booms in strip-clearing development began. The freezing rain continued well into the evening, thickening the coats of ice already on the trees, mostly very tall and somewhat fragile Southern pines. Hundreds of thousands of them were brought crashing down all around the city, while hundreds of power-line transformers overloaded and exploded throughout the night. By morning on January 8, some parts of the area had as much as four inches of solid ice coating everything, over two hundred thousand residences and businesses were without power, and most streets were completely impassible. The Georgia Power Company and other local power utilities quickly brought in crews from as far away as Texas and Virginia to deal with the disaster, working first to reconnect power to hospitals and nursing homes that had been relying on generators since the crisis began. When the crews began moving into the suburbs, they faced two problems, the still tree-littered and almost completely blocked side streets, and the thousands of snapped-off telephone and power poles that had to be rebuilt before any power could be restored. Most of these crews worked heroically, averaging eighteen to twenty hours a day in subfreezing and icy conditions; several were injured by falling ice and trees or by falls from poles when their spikes would not hold in the frozen wood. It took over two weeks to completely restore power to all the metro area. The stores that were able to reopen in the first days after the storm quickly depleted their stock, deliveries being impossible until the roads were cleared.

The 1973 storm and its lessons about preparations might have been forgotten if similar storms in the following decades had not repeated its effects. A rare daytime snowstorm on January 12, 1982, had also not been accurately forecast; what was supposed to be a light snowfall in the late evening hours began instead with a sudden heavy and sustained snowfall around noon when most businesses were still open and resulted in one of the worst traffic jams the city has ever witnessed later that afternoon. Temperatures rose just above freezing before plummeting, and the snowbound streets quickly took on a thick glaze of undrivable ice just as thousands of commuters were trying to make their way home. Another storm in 1992 resulted in as much as eighteen inches of snow falling in less than three hours over parts of the northern metro area; once again it quickly turned to ice in the streets of Atlanta. An unusual and again misforecast December snowstorm struck just before Christmas 2010, fortunately leaving the roads passable and bread and milk supplies at a normal level in the stores, while providing the city with its first white Christmas since 1882. Another storm just two weeks later, however, did deplete the stores of milk and bread, proving to be one of the worst to ever hit the city. For once well forecast and unfolding pretty much as expected, the monster storm came in on the Sunday night of January 9, 2011, bringing in upwards of eight inches of snow and another half inch or more of ice over the next three days. Business and travel came to an absolute standstill. Unlike the 1973 storm, however, this one was primarily a snow event, and while it did disrupt the city for over a week, power outages and structural damage were relatively minor.

THE ATLANTA CHILD MURDERS

1979–1981

In the summer of 1979, a series of murders and abductions began in south and southwestern Atlanta, mostly involving teenaged boys. Although the first two victims were discovered very close to each other on the same day, Atlanta police were slow to connect the cases, and even after more bodies turned up on subsequent days, were also slow to come to the realization that a serial killer was loose in the poorest neighborhoods of the city. In the end, the list of victims officially linked to a single killer numbered twenty-eight in a two-year period; the only things they shared in common were their race and violent deaths. The suspect finally brought to justice was only convicted of killing two of them, both adults.

Children do go missing frequently in America, especially in a large urban setting like Atlanta, to the tune of a staggering eight hundred thousand reports filed annually with police departments across the country. However, fewer than 120 of these each year are actual "stranger on stranger" criminal abductions with intent to do harm, so an initial report of children missing usually attracts little attention from the police. Atlanta police began to pay attention, however, a few weeks after July 28, 1979, when the body of thirteen-year-old Alfred Evans was found in a patch of woods off Niskey Lake Road in the Ben Hill area of west Atlanta. He had been missing for three days, apparently murdered by strangulation the day he disappeared. While investigating the scene, police discovered another body only fifty feet away, fourteen-year-old Edward Smith, who had been missing for seven days. Smith had died of a small-caliber gunshot wound, probably a .22 pistol round. Both boys were alleged to be frequent marijuana users and to have been at a "drug party" the week before; police speculated that their deaths were possibly linked through some drug deal gone wrong and initially performed only a superficial investigation.

The body of a third victim, fourteen-year-old Milton Harvey, did not surface until November 16, but he disappeared while riding his bike to the bank to pay a bill for his mother on September 4; his bicycle was found a week later on little-traveled Sandy Creek Road next to the Fulton County Airport. Harvey's skeletal remains were discovered eleven miles away in a trash dump off Redwine Road in East Point. As the remains showed no sign of struggle or injury, his death was not initially ruled a homicide. A fourth victim, Yusef Bell, disappeared after Harvey; his was the disappearance that finally convinced police that they had a serial killer loose in the city. Nine-year-old Bell had left home on October 21 to buy some items at a local store for a neighbor; he was seen leaving the store but never made it home. His mother, Camille Bell, unlike the earlier victims' family members, made high-profile appeals in the local media for her son's abductor to free him and constantly badgered the police to keep his case open and active. Bell's remains were found on November 9 in the abandoned E. P. Johnson Elementary School, wedged into a hole in the concrete flooring. He had been strangled and his feet were barefoot as they had been when he left home. An observant detective noticed, however, that they had been cleaned before his body was dumped. Due primarily to Camille Bell's high profile during the search, Yusef's funeral was a huge media spectacle, with most city leaders attending, including Mayor Maynard Jackson, the first black mayor of Atlanta. Jackson promised that he would order a full police investigation of Bell's death, but it wasn't until Camille Bell and family members of the other murdered and missing victims created the "Committee to Stop Children's Murders" that the police were pressured into considering all of the cases together. In July 1980 the formation of a multijurisdictional task force to investigate the murders was announced, with one of their first tasks to decide which of the dozens of disappearances and murders reported were in fact linked. Roughly ninety cases over the two-year period were connected by geographical or other factors with each other, but in the end only twenty-eight were deemed to have probably been committed by a single perpetrator. "The List," as the local media dubbed it, became deeply controversial at the time, and remains so today, both because of the disparate cases that were included on it and the strikingly similar cases that were not.

When the realization dawned in the community that numerous young black boys were being murdered, the ancient specter of the Ku Klux Klan reared its head, helped along by the news media's knee-jerk reactions. The FBI had successfully infiltrated the ranks of the KKK throughout the 1960s and 1970s in a program called COINTELPRO, to the point that there was, allegedly, a rally held in the late 1970s in which every Klansman present was either an undercover agent or informant. The FBI let the Atlanta task force know about a secret wiretap of Atlanta-area Klansmen who had discussed the murders approvingly; one of them, Charles Sanders, had previously threatened to "strangle" a child on the list because he had damaged Sanders's car while riding a go-kart. This was the only evidence that could be found to link the KKK to the murders. Another factor tended to exclude the old Klan—the way the bodies were found. Historically, the Klan was never an organization to hide its lynchings; instead of hiding the bodies in woods or rivers, where most of those on the list had been found, the Klan's preferred method would have been to hang them in the most prominent spot possible in the middle of the city. The fact that each of the victims had disappeared from his own poor, urban, and almost exclusively black neighborhood also made it unlikely that an older, white male presence would have gone unnoticed among the neighbors.

The widespread assumption that the Klan or some other white group or person had to be involved in the murders has never gone completely away, even thirty years after most of the cases were closed. As a result, politics played an even greater role than in most highly publicized murder investigations, creating a charged atmosphere in which the KKK and other white supremacists were blamed for the killings. To complicate matters, several victims included on the list seemed to have no connection to the other cases. Most serial killers are white men, but most also have patterns that did not fit this list of victims; they tend to prefer a single type of victim with consistent hair coloring, body composition, race, and age. Most serial killers are also either ritualistic or "disorganized" in the commission of murder; their murders are either conducted in a more or less identical fashion or they are committed with little forethought and in hasty, improvised ways. The victims on the list were all over the spectrum, twenty-six males from nine to twenty-eight years old and two females. Most simply disappeared from the streets but at least one was abducted from her bedroom. Some were shot, others stabbed, most were strangled, and still others beaten to death. Some had clothes missing, some had clothing on that didn't belong to them, some showed signs of ritualistic treatment or abuse, some were found dumped on trash piles, some were found in buildings, others in patches of woods, and still others in rivers.

The list of victims grew to sixteen by the late summer of 1980, but the task force seemed to be making little progress. Mayor Jackson formally asked the FBI for assistance. John Douglas and Roy Hazelwood of the FBI's Behavioral Science Unit were sent to give intelligence support to the investigation, and they quickly built a profile that proved controversial within the task force itself. The FBI investigators surmised that the killer was not in the Klan or in any organized hate group and was probably black. They speculated that he was twenty-five to twenty-nine years old, single, and closely watched media reports of the crimes. He had an authoritarian but casual relationship with children that would make them trust him enough to get into his car voluntarily. He probably worked in the music or entertainment business, probably lived on or near Memorial Drive, and had some sort of relationship with a police organization, probably as a civilian and not as a sworn officer. He would not only continue kidnapping and murdering but would also change his patterns in response to media reports. Further, they felt that not all the cases on the list were in fact linked.

Eleven-year-old Patrick Baltazar was found dumped in the woods off Buford Highway on February 6, 1981, the nineteenth body to be discovered. The next day, Atlanta news reports revealed that fiber evidence from the killer had been found on his body. Douglas and Hazelwood speculated that the killer had heard this and would change the location where he dumped his victims' bodies. He would probably throw them naked in a river to eliminate any traces of such evidence. The Chattahoochee River is the only large river flowing near Atlanta, and task force members supplemented by police academy recruits staked out each of its bridges for the next several months. With nothing turning up, the task force canceled the stake-outs on May 6. On the very last shift of the very last day, however, a police recruit named Bob Campbell, stationed at the South Cobb Drive bridge, heard a car stop above him at 2:30 a.m. Something was thrown over the rail that splashed into the water. He radioed to his backup team, who stopped the car as it was driving off the bridge. The man in the car turned out to be a twenty-three-year-old, single, freelance police news photographer and sometime music producer named Wayne Bertram Williams, who claimed he was on his way to Smyrna to audition a woman as a singer. Williams was from the Dixie Hills neighborhood of southwest Atlanta, close to the western extension of the Memorial Drive corridor. The woman he claimed to have been auditioning has never been found. Two days later, the nude body of twenty-seven-year-old Nathaniel Cater was found a few miles downstream; a forensic autopsy concluded he had been in the water somewhere between thirty-six and forty-eight hours. He became the twenty-eighth and final victim on the task force's list.

Williams was well known to the local police departments and television stations; he had worked as a freelance crime scene photog-rapher and had even testified for the prosecution in a capital murder trial. After Cater's body was discovered, police obtained a search warrant for Williams's home; the FBI interrogated and polygraphed him on the same day. The search of his car and home turned up numerous "foreign" fibers, hairs, and clothing fragments from people not living in the home, and police took a broad sample of fibers for forensic testing. These became key pieces of evidence in the ensuing trial, the first time such use of "microscopically identical" evidence was employed to convict a murder suspect. The polygraph results, by then not permissible to use in trial as evidence, nonetheless showed that Williams was evasive and not truthful in his answers about Cater's murder and disposal. Williams was arrested on June 19,

1981, for the single murder of Nathaniel Cater. He was, however, indicted by the Grand Jury on two counts of murder on July 17, the bill also including a charge for the murder of another adult on the list, Jimmy Payne. His trial began on January 6, 1982. Williams was never formally charged with the death of any other victim on the list or for any child murders at all, but the prosecution was able to introduce evidence from those other cases, based on their similarities to the ones he was charged in. Williams's defense was largely based on creating doubt in the jurors' minds that he was a person capable of such acts, but during a harsh cross-examination by the prosecution, Williams exploded in anger on the stand, showing just what a deceptively peaceful personality he in fact had. This exhibit of deep-seated anger, plus the mountain of scientific evidence, proved to be the deciding factors in the case. After just eleven hours of deliberation, the jury returned guilty verdicts on Saturday, February 27, 1982. Williams was sentenced to two consecutive life sentences.

After all the years of debate and speculation, key evidence was reexamined in the summer of 2007 that established a connection between Williams and one of the child victims. Two human hairs had been found inside Baltazar's shirt, which were determined at the time not to be his own. At Williams's trial forensic experts testified that the hairs in question appeared to be similar to his hair, but they were unable to give a more definite analysis. In 2007 lawyers working for Williams petitioned the courts to allow some of the hair samples found on all of the 27 victims to be retested for DNA evidence, confident that they would prove to be from someone else. Instead, the two hairs found on Baltazar were shown to be consistent with Williams's hair, not definitively proving that they were his but providing 130-1 odds against their coming from any other person.

There were many doubts about Williams's guilt at the time, and they have not abated in the years since his conviction. Chet

Dettlinger, a private investigator once thought involved in the murders, published *The List* in 1983, which provided extensive and detailed information to prove that there were many more victims than the task force had included and that Williams was, at the very least, not the sole murderer. Douglas of the FBI, in his own book, *Mind Hunter,* made the same point very bluntly. Many of those who doubted Williams's involvement with any or all of the murders, however, did not rise to his defense. James Baldwin spent a great deal of time in his book, *The Evidence of Things Not Seen,* deriding the prosecution of Williams, the entire investigation, and even the trial itself, which he termed "untidy" and the verdict "dubious." However, even he seemed unnerved by Williams, later writing, "I am thankful not to have been on that jury. Someone described Wayne Williams's karma—for which I read aura—as terrifying. I would have described it as vindictive: somebody, as the old Sly and the Family Stone hit puts it, you'd just love to burn."

THE LIMELIGHT DISCO OPENS

1980

There is an upscale grocery store near the intersection of Peachtree Street and Piedmont Road, just down the street from Lenox Square Mall in the Buckhead section of Atlanta, which is still called the "Disco Kroger," though it is neither a disco nor a Kroger these days. It is called that not because it ever had a particular selection of in-store music to shop by, but because it was at one time adjacent to one of the most famous, and notorious, nightclubs in Atlanta, the Limelight.

The 1970s have been termed the "Disco Era" with some wistfulness and more than a bit of disdain. Both the era and the music were a backlash against the intensely political atmosphere of the 1960s, and an extension of the drug-fueled hedonism that marked some aspects of the previous decade. It doesn't seem to make sense that the sixties era lasted until about 1973 to 1975, while the seventies as a distinct era lasted from about 1975 to 1981, but human events and popular culture follow their own chronological reality. The sixties as a culturally distinct era began with the death of President John F.

Kennedy and the arrival of British pop rock music in the form of the Beatles and the Rolling Stones; it ended with the close of the protest period and the Vietnam War. The "Disco" seventies began with post-Vietnam economic downturns and the subsequent election of President Jimmy Carter, ending with the declared "death" of disco, the rise of New Wave and punk music, and the election of President Ronald Reagan. These few short years featured not only the heyday of disco as a widely popular phenomenon but also what some have dubbed the "death of fashion" era and the beginning of a national drug-and-sex-fueled culture.

Disco culture had an odd beginning. Nightclubs for music and dancing had their roots in the Prohibition-era "speakeasies," which featured boatloads of illegal liquor and hot jazz bands playing live, but clubs that revolved primarily around dancing to either live bands or records played by a "disc-jockey" (DJ) had their beginnings in the Nazi era in Germany. American jazz culture had reached Germany before the National Socialists came to power in 1933, and though it was officially and loudly banned by the Nazis as "decadent American filth," it found a home in underground clubs patronized by anti-Nazi young adults and teenagers self-dubbed "Swing Kids." After the German invasion and conquest of France in 1940, these underground clubs found a home among young jazz aficionados in Paris as well. Live bands attracted too much attention from the Gestapo secret police, so instead, DJ's spun jazz records in what became known as "discotheques."

A postwar incarnation of these DJ-centered clubs, the Whisky à Go Go, was opened in 1947 by Paul Pacine in Paris. It soon became one of the most popular clubs in town and a magnet for the newly emerging class of internationally known celebrities, later called the "jet set." The beginnings of American discos can be traced back to a frankly nasty little bar on West 45th Street in New York, the

Peppermint Lounge, opened in 1958. Its primary claims to fame were the introduction of go-go dancing and the launch of the wildly popular "twist" dance craze of the early 1960s. American celebrities of all stripes flooded into the dive, including First Lady Jackie Kennedy, who was so enamored of the joint that she hosted several "Peppermint Lounge" nights in the White House itself. With a few exceptions, though, the dance and celebrity-infested clubs did not catch on nationally for another decade.

On April 26, 1977, a new "megaclub" opened on West 54th Street in Manhattan at the site of the twenties-era Gallo Opera House and former CBS television studio, quickly becoming the most infamous and influential disco of them all, Studio 54. Four nightclub owners and investors combined to finance the club, Steven Rubell, Ian Schrager, Tim Savage, and Jack Dushey, but Rubell, already a noted club owner and "name" attraction for the glitterati, became both the public face and highly selective doorman for the immediately successful nighttime destination. Rubell's Studio 54 set the tone and defined what such clubs would almost invariably feature during the relatively brief disco era: packs of celebrities and celebrity watchers looking to see and be seen; celebration of open drug use and sex, with the stairwells at Studio 54 a popular gathering place for both; and a never-ending stream of music spun by DJ's who were celebrities in their own right. They were carefully selected to provide a primal beat that varied very little between songs, giving the cocaine- and phencyclidine-fueled, fashionably dressed dancers a constant soundtrack for the night. Rubell soon gained notoriety for his club's highly selective and arbitrary admission policy, ordering his doormen to choose random "nobodies" who caught their eye to join the crowds of beautiful people and celebrities inside.

The first megaclub in the South predated Studio 54, opening in 1974 on US 1 in Hallandale, between Miami and Ft. Lauderdale.

Peter Gatien purchased the club, initially known as Rumbottoms, in 1976, remodeled it, and renamed it the Limelight. It featured a large dance floor with an elevated DJ booth, glittery decor featuring over forty thousand strobes and spinning lights in at least three hundred rows, overpriced drinks at the large bar, and a stainless steel ceiling reflecting an eight-armed "octopus" of spinning lights dead center over the stainless steel floor. When the Miami Limelight burned to the ground in 1979, Gatien was already looking to open branches of his club in other cities. The first he chose was Atlanta.

By then Studio 54 was world renowned, and Gatien sought to outshine its excesses in every way. He rented out space in a moderate-size strip mall in Buckhead, well outside the downtown area. The space he chose had formerly housed the Harlequin Dinner Theatre, closed three years earlier, and was located next to a standard-issue grocery store, not the premier setting for a massively popular, celebrity-driven and drug-infested dance club. It opened in February 1980. Club "members" flashed their cards to the doorman, passed the club's pet tiger just inside the door of the street-level entrance, and then descended a large staircase straight down to a glass-topped and lit-up dance floor. Beneath the dancer's feet was a large fish tank with two sand sharks swimming around, presumably completely deaf after the first night. A one-hundred-thousand-watt sound system kept the groove beat on, while thousands of rotating lights, strobes, and a glittering mirrored ball hung from the ceiling. Six-foot-high speakers flanked the dance floor and became sought-after dance platforms for the more extroverted patrons. Confetti, "snow," and tons of sparkly glitter fell from vents in the ceiling, while near-naked "exciters" hired by Gatien shook their booties and encouraged the crowd to do the same. Gold cages containing dancers, and the occasional celebrity, descended from the ceiling, a nod to the old Peppermint Lounge. The back wall of the club featured a private VIP room and rows of curtained "privacy booths," which rapidly became notorious as places for sexual escapades and rampant drug use. A notorious Jacuzzi hot tub provided patrons with plenty of opportunities to take off their clothes as did the separate but connected movie theater, which featured pillows on the floor instead of seats.

Gatien also copied Rubell's strict access rules and policies, which were modified or changed at the whim of the doormen, and depended on the patrons' level of dress or, more important, their attitudes. With this contrived exclusivity in place, the disco quickly became the "in" place in Atlanta. Lines for admission three and four hours long stretched down Piedmont Avenue on weekends during its heyday. As expected, celebrities descended on the Limelight in droves, one in particular giving Gatien's club its biggest national headlines. In June 1981 a former runner-up in the 1959 Miss America beauty pageant and famed 1970s television spokeswoman for the Florida Citrus Commission, Anita Bryant, was in Atlanta and visited the Limelight. While there, she spent several hours dancing with a well-known gay rights activist, Russ McGraw. Bryant was under heavy fire from the media and political liberals at the time for her firm antigay stance, and pictures of her dancing at the Limelight with McGraw made front-page headlines across the country.

Gatien moved to New York to open another branch of the Limelight in 1983, handing the reigns of the Atlanta club to his brother, Maurice. Due in part to Maurice Gatien's lack of business acumen, and in part to the "death of disco," the club declined in popularity, closing for good in September 1987 after struggling for years as a rental facility. Gatien eventually opened other Limelight clubs in Chicago and London before returning to Atlanta to open yet another short-lived dance club in 1989. He was arrested in New York in 1996 on a number of racketeering and drug charges. Gatien was later acquitted of most of the charges, but was convicted of tax evasion. He served a short sentence and was deported in 2003 to his native Canada.

There was indeed a large, suburban-style supermarket next door to the Limelight that predated the nightclub, having opened in the Peachtree-Piedmont Crossing Shopping Center in 1976. That Kroger closed on May 30, 2008, reopening as another, more upscale market called Fresh Fare. The old mirrored ceiling ball from the Limelight hangs in the store's front foyer, and there is still a sign on the building heralding its glory days as the "Disco Kroger."

HOSEA WILLIAMS MARCHES IN FORSYTH COUNTY

1987

The last large civil rights march and the last large public gathering of robed Ku Klux Klansmen in the South occurred on the same day at the same location, in a small, somewhat rural town on the northern outskirts of the Atlanta metro area. Happening just nineteen years after Martin Luther King Jr. had been assassinated, and just nine years before the world's attention would be focused on the Atlanta Olympics, this event was highly controversial in the area and around the region and was widely covered by the national and international media at the time. It is still remembered as a central part of the historical legacy of the small, foothilled Forsyth County. And it all started with one of Martin Luther King's main lieutenants walking down a country road.

Forsyth County, like most of the rest of the South, has had a tumultuous racial history. The Atlanta race riots of 1906 were not isolated events; they reflected a growing animosity against black citizens and new immigrants, who challenged the real or perceived social and political mores of the region. In Cumming, the county seat and largest town in Forsyth County, a white woman, Ellen Grice, reported to the sheriff that a pair of unknown black men had assaulted her inside her mother's home on Wednesday, September 4, 1912. At that time, there were 658 black residents of the county, about 5 percent of the population. Several suspects were arrested, but the situation grew much uglier on Saturday, September 7, when a prominent black preacher named Grant Smith told a gathering at one of the Cumming black churches that Grice had "a reputation," lending doubt to her story. Smith was attacked later that day by an enraged white mob, then rescued by sheriff's deputies and put in protective custody in the town jail. Mob agitators stirred up the crowd, threatening to blow up the jail to get to Smith and to kill anyone else responsible for the crime against Grice, but the situation turned much worse the next day.

On Sunday September 8, a young white woman named Mae Crow was walking down a path through the woods in nearby Oscarville, where she was accosted, savagely beaten, and raped by a black teenager named Earnest Daniel Knox. Knox left her in the woods to die, but came back in the night with at least one other man; they raped her again. Mae was found the next morning and regained consciousness long enough to tell who had raped and assaulted her. She died of her injuries on September 23. Knox was arrested on the same day Crow was found and immediately confessed to the crime. Fearing mob violence, the sheriff had him moved to the Gainesville city jail, and then to the Atlanta jail. However, when four other men were charged with the same crime and arrested the following day, they were simply taken to the Cumming city jail. A mob soon gathered, broke into the jail, and lynched one of the four, Rob Edwards, beating him with crowbars and then hanging him from a telephone pole on the northwest corner of the courthouse square. The state militia had already been called out and was able to rescue the other three men from the lynch mob. Two of the men were not indicted but remained in custody as material witnesses. Knox and Oscar Daniel were tried on October 3 and found guilty after a one-day trial. Both were hung publically on October 25.

Following the trial and executions, white mobs roamed the county, warning all the remaining black residents to move immediately or else there would be further violence. About 1 percent of all land in the county was owned by black farmers; all of this was abandoned within a few weeks. Most black residents left without experiencing violence or further intimidation, though several black churches were burned and at least one home owned by a black family was blown up. After that, until 1987, there was no known black population in Forsyth County or several other north Georgia counties. A small level of racially based violence continued, however, mostly against unwary travelers passing through the county. The most serious of these incidents occurred in 1982, when a black Atlanta firefighter was shot while leaving a picnic at adjacent Lake Lanier. This period of relative calm, though, ended with yet another race riot breaking out on January 17, 1987.

In late 1986, a Cumming martial arts instructor named Chuck Blackburn, originally from San Francisco, had been motivated by the upcoming second anniversary of the national Martin Luther King Day holiday to propose and plan a "brotherhood march" through parts of the county to celebrate what he believed was its progress beyond its racially charged past. Nearly as soon as word got out of his plans, Blackburn began receiving telephoned death threats and other intimidation aimed at disrupting the march. He decided that the situation was too volatile to continue with his plans, but another martial arts instructor in nearby Gainesville, Dean Williams, took up the torch and continued with the plans, renaming the event the "anti-intimidation march," which was scheduled for January 17. One of Martin Luther King's main lieutenants during the civil rights struggles, Hosea Williams of Atlanta, was contacted and agreed to participate in the brotherhood celebration turned civil rights march, bringing to seventy-five the total number of people planning to attend the event.

The march did not go well. Forsyth County Sheriff Wesley Walraven had promised and delivered police protection for the short march, mostly on outlying country roads, but was overwhelmed by the number of counterdemonstrators. J. B. Stoner, newly released from jail after serving time for an Alabama church bombing, showed up to agitate the counterdemonstrators and their supporters. One of the north Georgia Klan leaders, Daniel Carver, had announced that about one hundred Klansmen would attend to protest the march, but an estimated four hundred rock-and-bottle-throwing robed and uniformed Klansmen and associates brought the march to a halt. Four marchers were injured, including Hosea Williams, hit in the head by a brick, and eight counterdemonstrators were arrested. Sheriff Walraven shut down the march in fear that his men would not be able to prevent lethal violence to the demonstrators, but promised Hosea Williams that if he would agree to stop then and come back the next Saturday, he would ensure the marchers' safety, no matter what it took. Williams agreed.

Walraven, a former Georgia State Patrol trooper and high school biology teacher, was one of the new breed of Southern sheriffs, and was not about to let such violence go unchecked in his county. However, his resources were very limited to carry out the promised protection. Forsyth County had a total population of thirty-six thousand that year; his own sheriff's department could field only twenty deputies, and the small Cumming city police department only ten officers. Typical for small, rural Georgia counties at the time, an all-volunteer fire department and a two-ambulance Emergency Medical

Service rounded out the emergency services for the residents. To give Walraven support and protect the rescheduled march on January 24, Governor Joe Frank Harris ordered 1,500 National Guard troops mobilized with riot gear, with the rest of the 11,500 member Guard to stand by in case they were also needed. The Georgia State Patrol sent 350 troopers, one-third of all its officers; 185 uniformed Georgia Bureau of Investigations agents arrived; several SWAT teams from around north Georgia arrived ready for battle; and police and sheriff's departments from Fulton, Cobb, and Gwinnett Counties sent groups of officers. Even forty armed forest rangers from the Department of Natural Resources showed up to supplement the overwhelming law enforcement presence. A total of nearly three thousand Guardsmen and police officers lined the streets of the new march route, providing a protective bubble from the Georgia Highway 400 exit on Highway 20 to the courthouse square about one-and-a-quarter miles away. Walraven himself led the protective detail at the front of the march.

The march participants and protestors represented both sides of the civil rights struggles. Besides Hosea Williams, the march was led by civil rights leaders Coretta Scott King; Joseph Lowery and Benjamin Hooks, both U.S. senators from Georgia; Sam Nunn and Wyche Fowler; Georgia Congressman John Lewis; Atlanta Mayor Andrew Young; Assistant U.S. Attorney General William Bradford Reynolds; comedian and activist Dick Gregory; and Democratic presidential candidate Gary Hart. Around ten thousand marchers had been expected, but at least twice that number showed up, traveling on 175 buses provided by MARTA, Atlanta's public transportation system. So many showed up that the march was delayed by several hours and finally started around 2 p.m. Well-seasoned veteran marshals arranged most of the participants in battalion array, having them link arms and march in complete silence so any disruption could be heard and responded to quickly. About a hundred pastors, community leaders, politicians, and businessmen from Cumming and the surrounding county welcomed the marchers at the courthouse.

Counterdemonstrators were far less organized and numerous; estimates of their numbers vary because it was hard to distinguish them from simple onlookers. In all they numbered around 1,000 to 1,500 of the estimated 5,000 people lining the route and the courthouse square. A local organization, the Forsyth County Defense League, part of Richard Barrett's far-right Nationalist Movement, invited Barrett to the counterdemonstration, as well as former Georgia governor Lester Maddox, who showed up to denounce the marchers as Communists and traitors. J. B. Stoner; David Duke, the former KKK Grand Dragon of Louisiana and aspiring presidential candidate; Frank Shirley, a former KKK official and then-leader of the Klan splinter group, the White Patriot Party; Don Black of Stoner's old National States Rights Party; Edward Fields, publisher of the violently anti-Semitic and white supremacist *Thunderbolt* tabloid newspaper; along with a couple of hundred or so robed Klansmen from Georgia, North Carolina, and Texas showed up to lend their support to the segregationist cause. The leaders of the two largest Klan factions in Georgia, Ed Stephens, the Georgia Grand Dragon of the Invisible Empire Knights of the KKK, and David Holland, the Grand Dragon of the Southern White Knights of the KKK, both warned their members not to attend the march, claiming it was an FBI setup to get them all arrested.

The march was anticlimactically peaceful despite the loud shouting and jeering of counterdemonstrators. Few violent injuries occurred among the marchers: The worst of these happened to a man hit by a cement block through his car windshield and a woman hit with a steel pipe. The only known death among the marchers was a man who suffered a fatal heart attack as the march started. A total of fifty-six arrests were made that day, none among the marchers themselves. Duke, Shirley, and Black were arrested when they attempted to lead their own countermarch up the same route, while other arrests were all for inciting to riot, reckless conduct, public drunkenness, obstruction, and weapons charges. Only seventeen of those arrested were from Forsyth County, and local residents were very quick to point out, accurately, that the vast majority of those opposing the march were not from the area itself.

It is difficult to say if the march truly led to the end of segregation in Forsyth County. In the decade afterward, the county experienced an explosion of growth, was named one of the top twenty fastest-growing counties in the United States throughout the 1990s and 2000s, and was designated the thirteenth wealthiest county per capita in the nation by 2008. One primary reason driving this growth was the rapid expansion of industries and business along the Georgia Highway 400 corridor, which connects Cumming to Atlanta, especially the dot.com businesses booming in the northern arc communities before the big bust of 2000. Today, Forsyth County is a well-populated and wealthy suburban "bedroom" community for Atlanta, with a population mix that is no different than other northern arc counties and communities.

There is not and probably never really was a true national organization of the KKK, though it still exists in the form of 180 or so small splinter groups with an aggregate membership perhaps as high as 8,000. Despite the widespread belief in some political and social circles that the Klan would radically expand after the election of President Barrack Obama in 2008, perpetuated without substance by the media, to date there has been no hard evidence of that occurring. Ironically, one month after the Forsyth County marches, the largest Klan organization remaining at that time lost a civil court case in Alabama six years after a young black man had been murdered by Mobile Klansmen in the last public lynching in America. This stripped the Klan of both its finances and assets.

MUHAMMAD ALI LIGHTS THE OLYMPIC TORCH

1996

The grand and elaborate ceremonial announcement on September 18, 1990, of the site of the 1996 Olympic Games, created equal parts controversy, irritation, and grand celebration. It was widely thought that the twenty-sixth Games of the modern Olympics, on the one-hundredth anniversary of their rebirth, should take place in their ancestral home, Athens, Greece. This assumption seemed to many to make Atlanta's bid moot. Instead, at 7:49 a.m. on that hot, bright, Tuesday morning, a large crowd gathered at Underground Atlanta screamed for joy at the announcement from Tokyo—Atlanta had the Games!

Up until the very moment of this announcement, Atlanta's bid to host the Olympic Games had been seen as a joke by most, and a long shot at best. The city was widely ridiculed in the mainstream media as being "second-tier." Worst of all, it had been a Confederate city 125 years previously. The press also declared Athens, Greece, as "the natural and most logical" choice for the centennial games, a point the Greek Olympic Committee seized upon, stating it had a "historical right due to its history" to be awarded the prize. This arrogant declaration not only offended English teachers but also did not win any accolades from the International Olympic Committee (IOC) and was likely one of the factors that, in the end, was held against Athens.

An Atlanta lawyer named Billy Payne had first come up with the idea of Atlanta hosting the Games in 1987, and though met with much skepticism all across the state and region, was a dogged and persuasive speaker on the topic. Atlanta Mayor Andrew Young, with his civil rights and United Nations ambassadorial credentials, signed onto the project fairly early, giving serious weight to the bid effort. With early corporate sponsorship offers coming from Coca-Cola and other major Atlanta businesses, the bid became much more viable and focused as the International Olympic Committee selection process ground on over the next three years. Still, the announcement in Tokyo that late summer day took nearly everyone involved, including members of the Atlanta Organizing Committee itself, by surprise.

The very first sign that this news would not be universally celebrated came from the announcer in Tokyo himself, International Olympic Committee president Juan Antonio Samaranch, who visibly flinched when he opened the envelope and scowled as he proclaimed the winner as "Aht-lan-tah." Samaranch had made it clear during the decision process that he placed Atlanta nearly last on the list of cities bidding, ironically, just above Athens, and that he did not consider it to be a large enough or appropriate enough venue to host the huge international spectacle. Selection committee members of his own IOC radically disagreed with him, saying in the aftermath of the selection announcement that they almost universally thought Atlanta was a great city to serve as the host, and that pre-announcement favorite Athens would have been a disaster with its ongoing political meltdown and lack of anything remotely resembling sufficient infrastructure. The Athens Organizing Committee responded with great outrage, accusing Atlanta of staging a great corporate conspiracy to steal the Games from them, and compounding their word choice offenses with scientific ignorance when one Athens newspaper declared, "the Olympic flame will not be lit with oil, but with Coca-Cola." Just for the record, this did not occur.

With the award of the Games came a massive preparation period in the city. A new grand stadium had to be built, cleverly designed to be partly torn down afterward and remodeled into a new baseball stadium to house the Atlanta Braves, Turner Field. A small city of dormitories for the athletes was built across North Avenue from Georgia Tech and was later turned into the first student housing for the downtown Georgia State University. A blighted area on the west side of the downtown Five Points area, near the headquarters for CNN and the Olympic venues at the World Congress Center, was completely overhauled and turned into Centennial Olympic Park, which proved to be a popular gathering spot during the games, and which helped spark a commercial resurgence in the area after the Games. In total, building and renovating fourteen separate venues in the city, along with sixteen other venues as far away as Miami and Washington, D.C., cost a total of $1.8 billion, with another $500 million in tax money spent on indirect costs, including street improvements and infrastructure upgrades. Payne's team was able to attract enough corporate sponsorship and sell enough event tickets not only to pay the entire cost but also to give Atlanta a net profit of $10 million after the Games.

A constant complaint about the Atlanta Games was their highly visible corporate sponsorships. One criticism, in particular, made much of the fact that Coca-Cola had exclusive rights to drinks available in Olympic venues. The facts that other Olympic Games had had nearly identical exclusive sponsorships, that Coca-Cola was both known and highly popular worldwide, and that it was one of Atlanta's largest corporate businesses didn't seem to mute the outrage. Even more outrage was directed at the city by the IOC itself, after sponsorships and permits for retail sales were issued to venders and corporations for non-Olympic venues that had not made "contributions" and thereby been granted Official Olympic Sponsorships by the IOC. The Atlanta committee responded that such businesses were part and parcel of a capitalist system, and that the city could better control their locations and merchandise by issuing such permits. For some days these issues were fought in full view of the public and press, exposing some of the less seemly aspects of the officially nonprofit Games, before the IOC decided to drop what had become an obviously losing battle.

The Games themselves officially started with the Opening Ceremony on July 19. These ceremonies, which date back to the 1908 London Games, are an oddity; they have almost nothing to do with the Games themselves. Since the 1984 Los Angeles Games, the ceremonies had become more and more a bizarre and wildly elaborate staging of incomprehensible symbolism leading up to increasingly fancier ways of lighting the official Olympic Flame Cauldron. Even so, the opening ceremony is the single most hotly sought after event at the Games. Atlanta pulled the stops out, in front of eighty-five thousand people packed into the sold-out stadium and approximately 77 million watching on television around the world. One part of the ceremony, which was less ethereal and symbolic, angered the IOC and international media to no end; several hundred cheerleaders and cloggers danced as thirty bright silver and chrome Chevy pickup trucks drove around the stadium in an ecstatic display of absolutely typical American enthusiasm; this was condemned, of course, as a crass display of unacceptably "hick" Southern values and culture. The IOC had tried to block the donated pickups from being included, as Chevrolet was not an Official Olympic Sponsor, but relented when the corporate logos on the trucks were covered up so as not to offend them. The European media's near-universal condemnation of the cheerleaders as "in questionable taste" did not go over well with the mass of American football fans, either.

Near the end of the opening ceremonies, a final surprise was revealed. For weeks speculation had been rampant about who would actually light the torch; guesses ranged from local athletes to political figures to civil rights figures. The torch procession ran very late, about three hours behind schedule, and had one unscheduled stop along the way. Olympic medalist E. J. Slater, carrying the torch down Auburn Avenue, walked it around the reflecting pool to the crypt of Dr. Martin Luther King Jr., paying a silent tribute to the slain civil rights leader. As the flame later entered the stadium near the conclusion of the four-hour ceremony, the last of the 800 bearers in Greece and 12,467 in the United States took over. The very last of the outside stadium runners was a four-time discus gold-medal winner, Al Oerter, who handed off the flame to heavyweight boxing great and Atlanta native Evander Holyfield, who ran the flame into the stadium through a secretly built underground tunnel that emerged in the center of the field. Track star Voula Patoulidou of Greece joined Holyfield for a lap around the track, then handed over the flame to four-time gold-medalist swimmer Janet Evans, who carried the flame another lap around the stadium, then up a long ramp to the base of the cauldron. Just before she arrived, a lone figure stepped out from the shadows at its base, heavyweight boxing great Muhammad Ali. He had not been seen in public in some time, and many were shocked at his transformation from the once proud, physically powerful pugilist proclaiming, "I am the greatest!"

His body swollen and hands badly trembling from the Parkinson's disease that had wrecked his once-proud body, Ali raised his torch in triumph to the thunderous applause of the audience, then lit a fuse with it, the spark from which traveled up the nine-story tower of the cauldron, setting it alight with a mighty whoosh.

Although on July 27 the Games were marred by a terrorist bombing in Centennial Olympic Park that killed two and injured over a hundred, they continued and two weeks of competition ended with another ceremony on August 4. At the closing ceremonies, Samaranch, a former friend and political ally of Spanish fascist dictator Francisco Franco, once again showed his animosity toward Atlanta, this time a bit more diplomatically. In his concluding remarks, he left out his otherwise universal praise in other Olympic Games, declining to say that they were "the best ever," and instead damning them with the faint praise of being "most exceptional."

AERIAL RESCUE AT
THE ATLANTA MILL FIRE

1999

Early on the morning of April 12, 1999, Ivers Sims left his home in the small Alabama town of Woodland, traveling the 132 miles up Interstate 85 to report to work. His office was a small cab atop a 225-foot-high Hammerhead crane at the site of a large renovation project in Atlanta's Cabbagetown neighborhood. Early that same morning, Firefighter Matt Moseley left his home in Locust Grove, south of Atlanta, driving the thirty-seven miles up Interstate 75 to report to work as a fire-rescueman assigned to Squad 4 of the Atlanta Fire Department, which was located in Station 4 on Ellis Street. By mid-afternoon, these two men's lives would collide in one of the most dramatic live scenes ever carried on Atlanta's local television stations.

Cabbagetown is just southeast of the central downtown district, at the former site of the famed Atlanta Rolling Mill, which was blown up by Confederate forces as they evacuated Atlanta in 1864. While the origin of the name is lost in the mists of time, it was once a thriving, working-class neighborhood; today it contains the bare remnants of a once-bustling mill village. Jacob Elsas, an immigrant from Germany by way of Cincinnati, arrived in the city in 1868, and soon set up a cotton bag and sack business at the old rolling mill location. Business boomed, and by the turn of the century, his Fulton Cotton and Bag Mill Company had become a large industrial complex, housing three separate large mills, several warehouses and associated smaller buildings, and a fair-size village for the mill workers. The mill attracted a large number of workers from the poverty-stricken mountain and mid-Georgia farming communities, giving the operation an overall Appalachian culture in the middle of the booming urbanized city. Changes in consumer goods and packaging materials led to the mill's decline after World War II; it finally closed its doors for good in 1978. The large industrial complex remained empty, save for trash, rusting heavy machinery, and derelicts, until 1997, when a development company purchased the property with an eye to converting some of the mill buildings into newly fashionable loft apartments for urban pioneers.

The Atlanta Fire Department dates to a single volunteer fire brigade, organized at a meeting in Addison Dulin's Store on Marietta Street, on February 2, 1848. The first recorded major fire in Atlanta occurred just two years later at a cotton warehouse on Alabama Street, which burned on April 15, 1850. Three other groups, all bucket-brigade-style organizations without any real equipment or training, soon joined this first company in the growing city. The need for both training and proper equipment and a real fire department organization became apparent after two women and two children lost their lives in a house fire on December 22, 1858, and the first Atlanta fireman was killed in action. Runner Levin S. Blake, of Engine Company 1, died while attempting to clear gunpowder away from a spreading store fire on April 13, 1859. The Atlanta Fire Department

(AFD), an all-volunteer incorporation, was formed in January 1860, consolidated from four of the independent fire brigades in the city: Atlanta Engine Company 1, Mechanic's Fire Department No. 2, Atlanta Hook and Ladder Company 1, and Tallulah Fire Company No. 3. The term "fire chief" was not yet in use; Atlanta's first Chief Engineer of the new department was William H. Barnes. Barnes was only on the job for two years. He resigned to take a commission in the Confederate army. Captain Barnes, the commanding officer of Co. A, "Leyden's Battery," 9th Battalion, Georgia Light Artillery, in Lee's Army of Northern Virginia, was mortally wounded in action during one of the last battles of the war, Saylor's Creek. He died of his wounds on May 10, 1865.

Atlanta's fire department operated exclusively manual engines at first, and large teams of strong-backed firefighters were needed to operate the pumps for as long as the water supply lasted or until the fire was out. Like almost everything else in the city, all the equipment was either confiscated or destroyed once Federal troops left in 1864. Unlike the horse-drawn engines seen in *Gone with the Wind* during the burning of Atlanta, all fire equipment in the city was moved around strictly by hand until 1867, when the first horses to draw the equally new steam-powered engines were obtained. After the war, the department was restarted in part with equipment donated by other cities and remained a fully volunteer force until July 7, 1882, when it was reorganized as a paid professional department under newly appointed Fire Chief Matthew Ryan.

A major fire in May 1917 that burned over 1,900 homes and displaced ten thousand residents transformed both the city landscape and the fire department. The immediate need for a serious upgrade to new equipment was made clear in the fire department's losing battle to stop the massive fires; the switch to all-gasoline-powered fire equipment was completed within a year. In May 1918 the fire department, now under Chief William B. Cody, staged a parade of its spanking new engines and ladder truck. Fourteen red-varnished and yellow-wheeled pieces of apparatus paraded down Peachtree Street draped in Red Cross banners as part of a bond drive; they marked the end of the horse-drawn engine era. Fire Chief John Terrell was appointed in 1929 and proved an exceptionally forward-thinking chief. He set up the first fire rescue company and organized the first formal fire academy for new recruits. Initially, training consisted of seventy-five hours of instruction in the rudiments of the job. On February 26, 1933, Terrell became the only Atlanta fire chief to die in the line of duty, killed in a car wreck en route to what proved to be a false alarm.

By 1999, the AFD had thirty stations, with another five stations at Hartsfield International Airport, manned by nearly a thousand firefighters. The department answered nearly sixty thousand calls in total that year, most companies responding on average once or twice per twenty-four-hour shift to trash fires, medical first-response calls, and far too many false alarms. On the early afternoon of the sunny but cool day of April 12, Moseley at Squad 4 was in the middle of a fairly routine day. Squads, formerly known as "Heavy Rescue" units, are the special operations forces of the fire department, trained and equipped for nearly any kind of situation that goes above and beyond what normal fire crews might encounter. Moseley was the hazardous materials specialist for his crew, put to work first thing that morning as they responded to a chlorine leak alarm. They were back at Station 4 by eleven a.m., and the next call came in at 2:37 p.m. That call, however, was anything but routine.

Sims arrived at the Fulton Mill construction site a little after seven a.m., and then made the long climb up to the cab of his crane. He usually had to take a break along the way, but remarked later that he hadn't that day; the wind was gusting and he wished he had put on an extra shirt to ward off the chill. He spent the rest of the morning helping other workers remove waterproofing materials from the roof of Mill No. 1, tons of gravel and tarpaper loaded onto a skid plate attached to his crane. Then Sims swung the load over to a trash bin outside the walls of the mill building. A little after 2:30 that afternoon, Sims had removed five loads, the tarpaper and gravel almost completely cleared, when he noticed smoke coming out of a hole in the roof. Workers below him found a small trash fire burning in a pile on the fifth floor and attempted to put it out with a number of fire extinguishers, but with the cold wind whipping through the structure at up to forty miles per hour, the situation quickly deteriorated. As flames burst through the hole in the roof, Sims called the workmen from his radio, "Y'all got a fire on top of the building!" The workmen quickly disappeared down an interior stairwell, as Sims suddenly realized he needed to get out of the area himself. Before he could even get up out of his chair, though, flames tore through the roof and wrapped around the base of the giant crane. Sims was trapped.

The first alarm was struck by AFD dispatch at 2:37 p.m., sending four engine companies, two ladder companies, a battalion chief, an air supply unit, and Moseley's Squad 4. First-in engine crews reported a large trash fire covering the fifth floor and already extending down to the fourth floor. As they were still setting up for an interior attack, with a second alarm struck and on the way, the fire grew explosively, forcing the fire crews to abandon the structure and run for their lives. A third and fourth alarm were struck nearly simultaneously, as mill houses started to burn from the scattering embers, and the fire increased rapidly in intensity. Over the next hour, three more alarms would be struck, the fireground situation deteriorating rapidly. Moseley and the other members of Squad 4 began kicking in the doors of the other burning structures, making sure no one had been left behind in any of the buildings and homes on the scene. Shortly after finishing, they heard a radio call to return to their unit to prepare for a rescue.

Retreating workmen had told the fireground commanders that their crane operator, Sims, was trapped in his cab, completely cut off by the roaring inferno, but the commanders' initial plan was to knock back the fire before getting him down. The rapid acceleration of the fire, and subsequent rapid degradation of the fireground, made that point moot. Squad 4 was going to have to come up with some sort of plan to get Sims out alive. It was very clear that they were not going to be able to do this from the ground, and the hunt was soon on for an available helicopter. A total of seven police and news helicopters were in the area, but all were either inadequate or too overloaded with equipment to assist in an aerial rescue attempt. Hearing the drama unfolding on WSB-TV, as the AFD's public information officer made a live plea for any available helicopter to assist, a Department of Natural Resources (DNR) Bell Long Ranger quickly prepared for takeoff from nearby Charlie Brown Airport in west Fulton County. The DNR had the only two dedicated rescue helicopters in the state, and pilot Boyd Clines was an experienced police and DNR pilot, as well as a veteran combat pilot in Vietnam. Clines and his crew chief Larry Rogers had the helicopter spun up and in the air within ten minutes.

Sims had to abandon the cab about thirty minutes after the fire began, as it had begun to burn from the intense radiant heat. He climbed on top of a pile of cement block counterweights at the far end of its horizontal beam, protected from the heat but completely helpless once the tower was heated to its failure and collapse point. As happened in the World Trade Center towers on 9/11, the fire was not hot enough to actually melt the steel of the structure but was well in excess of the temperature necessary to bring the tower's steel core to its structural failure point. Clines arrived and landed in a nearby field one hour and fourteen minutes after the fire had started. Moseley had been tagged as the rescueman, had already rigged himself with a full-body harness, and had assembled a rescue harness for Sims out of a twenty-foot length of one-inch flat webbing. Rogers had rigged two rescue lines from the helicopter's lift ring while they were en route, and Moseley was able to hook up in less than a minute after they arrived. Clines carefully flew upwind of the crane, buffeted by the strong winds gusting by then up to fifty miles per hour aloft, and was able to place Moseley, dangling eighty feet underneath, on the horizontal axis of the crane, just inboard from Sims, without incident. Once on the crane, Moseley quickly fastened the rescue harness on Sims, hooked him to the other rescue line Rogers had rigged, and in only one minute and thirty seconds after Moseley touched down, Clines safely lifted both off the crane. Less than fifteen minutes after the helicopter arrived, Sims was safely on the ground and being loaded into an ambulance.

The rescue of Sims seemed quite anticlimactic, but only because the entire team involved was the model of quiet professionalism. Moseley was an immediate hero in the eyes of Atlantans, and by the next morning the whole nation. The entire rescue sequence was shown live on every local television channel. The fire was another story, proving to be one of the most complex and difficult operations the fire department had encountered that decade; a massive show of manpower was needed to bring the inferno under control. Seven alarms were sounded in the end, bringing sixteen engine companies, thirteen ladder companies, fifteen other companies, and 155 fire and EMS personnel to the scene. The fireground itself was huge and complicated; seven other separate fires in other structures were started by the initial blaze, and the complex nature of the industrial buildings meant that fifteen different command sectors had to be established.

The Atlanta Fire Department had come a very long way since its mid-eighteenth-century origins as a casual, untrained volunteer force. No one was killed in the incident and, fortunately, only relatively minor injuries were suffered by any of the Atlanta firefighters, but hot spots and reignites continued for the next week in parts of the complex. The fireground was finally closed at 1:49 p.m. on April 20, almost exactly eight days after the small trash fire began.

THE GHOSTS IN THE LAB

2001

It was a clear and cloudless warm Tuesday morning in late summer, with all the makings of a really beautiful day. The William B. Hartsfield Atlanta International Airport hummed along as usual, recently named as the busiest airport in the world. With a new fifth runway under construction, it was set to handle even more traffic in the years to come. A few miles north next to the campus of Emory University, researchers at the Centers for Disease Control and Prevention, the CDC, continued monitoring a new study involving monkeys infected with a deadly and dangerous disease, expecting a routine and somewhat boring day. It was September 11, 2001.

The CDC was originally organized in Atlanta in 1946, in the downtown location of the wartime Malaria Control in War Areas office. It was intended from the beginning to be a peacetime, civil organization under the U.S. Public Health Service, with no formal ties to the military. From its original task of eradicating malaria from the southeastern United States, especially around the many military bases training men for the war effort, in the late 1940s, it progressed to investigating disease outbreaks and disseminating information about them to health practitioners. When threats of biological warfare occurred in the early 1950s during the Korean War, the CDC widened its focus to include these potential problems along with its monitoring of potential outbreaks of natural diseases. Emory University offered the CDC space on its campus along Clifton Road, giving the young agency room to expand its operations and laboratories there in the late 1950s.

Three high-profile efforts gave the CDC its reputation as an effective protector of the public health. In the mid-1950s, its labs identified problems with contaminated Salk vaccines that were causing illnesses in children and ran the fix to the immunization program. That same decade, a widespread outbreak of influenza was prevented from becoming a pandemic largely as a result of the CDC's development of the first influenza vaccine. Then, starting in 1962, CDC researchers and field scientists set up a monitoring, containment, and vaccine program that ended up eradicating the world's most virulent and lethal disease, smallpox. By late 1977, for the first time in human history, no cases of smallpox were found anywhere in the world, and the disease was declared eliminated in 1979. Smallpox was thought to have originated in the earliest human populations and had been responsible for upwards of 500 million deaths in the twentieth century alone. While other diseases had a higher mortality rate than smallpox's 60–80 percent, none had more longevity or ability to spread among differing populations than the *Variola major* virus, the formal name of the most common type of smallpox.

By the late 1990s, with the rise of Islamic terrorism and its potential use of biological weapons against civilian populations, the CDC partly returned to its military roots, working on programs with its Defense Department counterparts to prepare for such attacks. One of the specific areas of research in this antiterrorism effort was highly controversial both inside and outside the agency. With the elimination of the smallpox threat, researchers had been divided on what to do with the remaining samples of live *Variola*. In the 1990s, the World Health Organization, or WHO, had organized an effort to concentrate all the known samples in only two locations in the world, the Maximum Containment Laboratory at the CDC and the Russian State Center for Research on Virology and Biotechnology, in Koltsovo, Russia; it had begun talks about the advisability of destroying those stockpiles as well. The last samples of the tiny *Variola*, the biggest killer of mankind since time immemorial, would hopefully end up as ghosts in those laboratories, faint echoes of the most perfect killing machines ever created.

Many CDC researchers were heartily in support of destroying the samples to ensure that they would not become a source for any future outbreak. Other researchers argued just as heartily that it was essential to preserve samples of live *Variola,* so vaccines could be created in the case of future outbreaks, natural or engineered, of the incredibly lethal disease. Everyone agreed, though, that smallpox in the wild had really and truly been eliminated and assumed that the only known sources available were in the American and Russian labs. In late 1989, however, the first crack in this assumption was created by one Vladimir Pasechnik, the former director of the Soviet Institute for Ultrapure Biopreparations in St. Petersburg, who took the opportunity at a conference in Paris to defect. He was deeply, personally disturbed at some of the work being done at his own facility and wanted to let the Western world know of it. The Soviets had not only failed to concentrate their stockpile of smallpox samples in one, well-guarded laboratory but they were also "heating it up," making it more virulent, and reproducing it by the ton at other laboratory facilities for the specific purpose of using it as a weapon.

This ground-shaking revelation was enough to end any further attempts at *détente,* but came so late in the Communist empire's day that diplomats were unable to get involved before the Soviet Union itself collapsed two years later. Rather than end the threat, the empire's collapse spread it. Formerly well-guarded Soviet bases and laboratories became open and easy pickings for anyone who wished to steal pretty much anything from them, from fighter aircraft to tanks to submarines, all the way down to small ampules containing lethal smallpox *Variola.* With terrorism on the rise around the world, these small ampules would fetch premium prices. And ex-Soviet scientists, some nearly on the verge of starvation after not being paid for months, were only too happy to sell whatever the market desired to the highest bidder.

The arguments to destroy remaining stockpiles continued through the 1990s, the massive Soviet stockpiles being conveniently forgotten by the factions wanting the samples gone. In July 1999 the WHO decided to keep the samples available for research until 2002, unless something was found in the meantime that would warrant their continued existence. Peter Jahrling and John Huggins of the U.S. Army Medical Research Institute of Infectious Disease, or USAMRIID, began a new series of experiments to develop a human vaccine, but lacking any smallpox *Variola* to experiment with, had to get the CDC to share its samples and labs in the effort. While their own work was underway, Jahrling discovered that Australian researchers had succeeded in doing what the Soviets had been rumored to have achieved; they used a simple genetic modification to make a "superpox," one that is resistant to any vaccine, and that could, potentially, spread like wildfire through human populations. Although the Australians had achieved this with a genetically similar but nonlethal variant called mousepox, the implications were clear. The tools were easy to use; any undergraduate college student with a smattering of knowledge in biological laboratory procedures could pull it off with an inexpensive kit available on the Internet, and some terrorist groups like al-Qaeda were wealthy enough, inhumane enough, and motivated enough to use these. Osama bin Laden and his allies had already shown their willingness to use any weapon available to them, and as "peripheral casualties" was not a term they recognized, were not deterred by the idea of releasing a "superpox" on any given population they chose. The race was on to see if it was really possible to make superpox into a deployable weapon, and then to see what could be done to prevent its use or respond in the event of its release. On May 30, a USAMRIID team led by Jahrling and Huggins set up shop in a basement corridor of one of the CDC buildings next to the Maximum Containment Laboratory. They began a new set of experiments on the possibility of "heating up" lethal smallpox *Variola*.

By early September, their experiments had already shown some disturbing results; they had been able to transmit human smallpox to monkeys, once thought to be impossible. They were preparing to extend these into trials with potential vaccines. On the morning of September 11, their Maximum Containment Laboratory was filled with caged monkeys exposed to smallpox and at different levels of infection. One had died the day before and a researcher was beginning to perform a necropsy on its body. Just after nine a.m., one of the researchers, Sergeant Rafael Herrera, was listening to a radio inside his level-five containment suit, when he heard the news. Turning to the other researchers, and unable to speak to them through the pressure suits and over the noise of air hoses, he wrote on a piece of paper, "A plane crashed into the World Trade Center."

The nation's worst terrorist attack began at 8:46 a.m. on September 11, when American Airlines Flight 11 crashed into the World Trade Center (WTC) North Tower (also called Tower 1), followed by United Flight 175, which was flown into the South Tower, or Tower 2, at 9:03 a.m.. The second crash occurred in front of a worldwide live audience on the televised morning news shows. At 9:37 a.m. American Airlines Flight 77 was flown into the Pentagon's western wall, while United Flight 93 crashed near Shanksville, Pennsylvania, at 10:03 a.m. after passengers attempted to seize control of the plane from the hijackers. This flight had been heading toward Washington, D.C., and the U.S. Capitol building. Federal Aviation Administration (FAA) controllers knew they had a serious problem on their hands, with at least one airliner known to have been hijacked even before the first WTC tower was struck, and had requested help from the North American Air Defense Command, or NORAD, at 8:37 a.m. Just one minute after United Flight 175 crashed into the second tower, the FAA began shutting down airspace, initially in the New York to Boston corridor, but expanding to an unprecedented nationwide ground stop order at 9:45 a.m., while the Air Force scrambled every fighter available to counter what was obviously a massive coordinated attack.

In Atlanta, controllers were monitoring the situation and immediately closed the airport when the ground stop order was given, allowing planes on approach to land, but turning back every departing flight to gates at the terminal. There were 3,395 commercial aircraft in the air when this order was given; every one was ordered to land forthwith at the nearest available facility. Long-term residents of Atlanta are well familiar with the usual flight paths of landing and departing aircraft, and undoubtedly some of the landing flights coming in on little-used and unfamiliar air routes caused confusion and some level of panic. In the containment lab, Herrera was continuing to listen to radio reports, and writing out updates on his pad to his colleagues in the room, when someone banged on the glass window to the outside hallway, holding up a sign reading,

"You need to evacuate." Officials in Washington knew of the small-pox experiments going on at the CDC, and concerned that another hijacked plane might crash into the facility, potentially releasing the lethal *Variola* into the neighboring residential areas, called the CDC's director and ordered him to shut them down. The problem was that they not only had a freezer full of deadly samples in the room but they also had a highly contagious monkey body, and other live, infected monkeys that could spread their contagion. In the best of circumstances, it would take up to a half hour to shut down their experiments and decontaminate themselves enough to safely get out of the facility. Time ran out, the CDC staffer came back up to the window, this time holding up a sign stating, "Emergency Procedures." Rumor had spread that a plane had been hijacked from Hartsfield airport and was heading toward the CDC at that moment. Pulling emergency handles, hundreds of gallons of harsh disinfecting chemicals poured over them and their smallpox-exposed, level-five suits as they pushed the crash-exit bars to the outside doors, running out of the most lethal space in the world into an open parking lot.

As it turned out, the rumor a plane was headed toward the CDC was false, but the rumor of a planned attack on Atlanta was not. Details of whatever is known about this plan are classified, but one startling fact did leak out to the media. After planes that had taxied back to the Hartsfield terminal after the ground stop had been emptied, cleaning crews had extra time to clean and maintain them, as the ground stop stayed in place for three days before being gradually lifted. As maintenance workers cleaned and prepared a Delta aircraft that had been stopped before taking off from its scheduled flight to Brussels that morning, they found two box cutters taped up under seats, similar to the reported weapons hijackers on the four doomed flights had been armed with during the attacks.

THE FIRST ATLANTA TORNADO

2008

While the South is well known for its violent weather, and frequent tornadoes have occurred in every month of the year, downtown Atlanta had never been struck directly by one. The city had lived a charmed existence since its founding in 1845, and seemed topographically advantaged against the wrath of storms, perched above the surrounding terrain on a low ridge running roughly northeast to southwest. This ridge seemed to funnel the worst weather either to the western counties, which had indeed been more frequently ravaged, or to the eastern counties, which suffered fewer but more lethal storms over the years. This exclusion from the tornado victims' club ended on the late evening of Friday, March 14, 2008.

While tornadoes can and have developed during any month of the year, the prime season in Atlanta is from early March through early June. A tornado is a complex weather event, usually formed at the trailing edge of a powerful, rotating convective storm cell as it draws in warm, moist air and collides with cooler dry air aloft. If these colliding air masses hit at just the right time, angle, and manner, they wrap together, spinning like an ice skater on the tip of one blade, gaining more energy and momentum as more warm and cool air rushes into the growing system. The exact mechanics of how the phenomenon develops are still unknown, but about 1,200 times a year in the United States, these cyclonic storm systems develop into tornadoes, reaching wind velocities up to 300 miles per hour on the ground, and creating paths of destruction up to two-and-a-half miles wide and up to 219 miles long. As solar heating seems to play a large role in the formation of these storms, they usually form in the middle to late afternoon of unusually warm days in the spring and early summer. Some have struck in the morning hours, however, and the most terrifying have formed late at night, when darkness cloaks their course and lethality. Tornadoes come in a variety of sizes and forms, but are rated by their strength according to the Fujita Scale, which ranges from F0 (40–78 miles per hour) to F5 (261–317 miles per hour). A newer system reflecting new discoveries about true wind velocities inside the tornado's funnel, the Enhanced Fujita Scale, uses an EF0–EF5 rating with somewhat lower wind values.

At one time the prevailing wisdom was that tornadoes would not go through a heavily built-up urban area, primarily because there had been none observed throughout the nineteenth and twentieth centuries. The supposition was that the "heat island" developed by large cities—a phenomenon in which cities are frequently several degrees warmer than their immediately surrounding suburbs—somehow reduced the energy of a storm system (though the direct opposite would be a more logical conclusion!), and that storm cells were somehow broken up by the tall buildings, which disrupted cyclonic wind patterns. This theory was put to rest in a dramatic fashion in Salt Lake City on August 11, 1999, when an F2 tornado roared right through the middle of downtown. That storm also put to rest the theory that storms of such magnitude were unlikely to strike that far west in the arid parts of the continental United States. It resulted in the second death from a tornado in Utah's history; the first was in 1884.

That Friday in March had been a clear and warm day in Atlanta; rain was predicted for the late afternoon and evening. This was welcome news, as the region had been locked in a deep drought for quite some time, and there were already worries about water supplies for the upcoming, normally dry, summer. A Southeastern Conference (SEC) college basketball tournament between Alabama and Mississippi State was going on in the large, sprawling, and solidly packed Georgia Dome on the west side of downtown, an NBA basketball game was going on in nearby Philips Arena, and the normal Friday night crowds wandered around the downtown area. The National Weather Service's Storm Prediction Center (SPC) in Norman, Oklahoma, had been following a number of storm cells advancing through the southeastern states throughout the afternoon, and concerned that they were growing more powerful than predicted, issued a "slight risk of severe weather" alert at 9:00 p.m. Atlanta was included in the warning area, but the SPC initially gave it just a 2 percent chance of experiencing dangerous weather. Individual storm cells were drifting across the western part of the state, but had not formed into a dangerous squall line, a typical tornado-producing formation common during this time of the year. With the absence of squall lines, and no growth expected in the coming storm clouds, no storm watches or warnings had been issued for the area that evening. This changed rapidly; as the sun began setting, one of the larger storms coming in from Alabama blew up rapidly into a supercell, the most powerful type of thunderstorm, and at 9:26 p.m., a tornado warning was sounded for Cobb County, Fulton County, and Atlanta itself, a "hook" echo typical of tornado formation showing up on radar as just six miles northwest of downtown.

With no earlier warning that bad weather could occur that evening, most people in the downtown area were caught completely by surprise, and many were still out in the open spaces of Centennial Olympic Park and nearby Underground Atlanta. At 9:38 p.m., a powerful tornado, later rated as an EF2 with at least 130-mile-per-hour winds, touched down in Vine City west of the Georgia Dome, tracked rapidly just north of it, and almost directly through the adjacent Georgia Word Congress Center, heavily damaging both of the occupied buildings. It then went directly through the CNN/Omni Hotel Complex and adjacent Philips Arena and tracked across the northern portion of Centennial Olympic Park toward the hotel district. The tornado stayed on the ground, tearing through the heart of downtown and striking or glancing off three large skyscrapers, the Equitable and Georgia Pacific Buildings, and the round tower of the Westin Peachtree Plaza Hotel, as well as damaging nearly every other building along its path. Typical of southeastern tornadoes, the funnel cloud lifted off the ground briefly as it crossed the I-75/85 Downtown Connector, then grounded again in the residential and light commercial areas east of downtown, grinding eastwards another mile before weakening and falling apart over western DeKalb County.

Damage was immense in the downtown area, with the Omni and Peachtree Plaza Hotels losing many of their windows and suffering light structural damage, and the Georgia Dome's roof damaged and partially torn off. The Peachtree Plaza was also reported to have swayed up to two feet at its seventy-third top floor from the brute force of the storm; fortunately, it had been designed to do so instead of collapsing. Historic Oakland Cemetery on the east side of downtown was directly hit, suffering a great deal of damage to the monuments and landscaping. CNN's studios were damaged, though the cable news channel stayed on the air throughout the incident, water falling on the side of the anchor desk from holes in the roof.

Centennial Olympic Park lost two of its distinctive Hermes light towers and was thoroughly covered by broken glass and debris from the nearby damaged buildings. Many other businesses and homes were damaged, but one casualty that struck the heart of lifelong Atlantans in particular was the Atlanta Dairies plant on Memorial Drive, east of downtown. Already scheduled to be closed later in the year, it lost most of its roof in the storm. This forced an early end to the beloved business that was the site of so many school field trips over the years; it had provided a hometown favorite brand in the years before the national brands sold in giant supermarkets took over.

The tornado also tore through the old Fulton Cotton and Bag Mill in Cabbagetown, scene of a dramatic rescue during a fire in 1999. It had been renovated into loft apartments and was partly occupied at the time, but the tornado heavily damaged all seven buildings on the site, causing partial building collapses and roof cave-ins that resulted in a complex and lengthy search by fire-rescue crews. Although there were reports of people trapped in an elevator and one person was still missing after more than twenty hours of operations, in the end only one firefighter was injured, and the missing person was later located elsewhere.

With all the widespread damage, human casualties were surprisingly light; only about twenty people were injured badly enough to seek treatment in the area hospitals. At first, it was thought that no deaths had resulted from the tornado, but a week later, as workmen were clearing away bricks from a wall that had collapsed across the street from the Martin Luther King Jr. MARTA Station, they discovered the body of a homeless man. He had apparently sought shelter from the storm alongside the now-collapsed building located next to a parking lot on Decatur Street, and according to an autopsy, died instantly when the wall fell on him. He was not carrying any identification, and no one had reported him missing. He has never been identified.

ATLANTA FACTS AND TRIVIA

- Downtown Atlanta sits astride the Eastern Continental Divide. Rain that falls west of Peachtree Street flows to the Chattahoochee River and eventually to the Gulf of Mexico. Rain that falls east of Peachtree drains to a series of rivers, eventually emptying in the Atlantic Ocean.

- There is no "Tara Plantation" in Georgia. It is a fictional location in Margaret Mitchell's book, *Gone With the Wind,* based on her mother's experiences on a real plantation in Clayton County, Georgia. Real antebellum mansions, like the one her maternal grandmother, Annie Fitzgerald Stephens, was born in, looked nothing like the movie version, either.

- Margaret Mitchell apparently did not think well of the house where she lived for seven years and where she wrote *Gone With the Wind,* frequently referring to it as "the dump." Empty and abandoned by 1977, it was set on fire twice, probably by vagrants, before being purchased and renovated in 1995. It burned again during renovations, completely gutted just days before it was to open as a museum dedicated to Mitchell and the book. Now on the National Register of Historic Places, it has since been reopened as a museum and literary center operated by the Atlanta History Center. Docents state that the nickname was Mitchell's "affectionate" reference to the house.

- Although beloved by his men, Confederate General Joseph Eggleston Johnston was not thought of as highly by the Confederate high command and government officials. It may be for that reason that there was for many years only one statue of the diminutive defensive-warfare genius anywhere in the United States, near the downtown square in Dalton. A second statue was erected in 2010 on the Bentonville, North Carolina, battlefield, where he made his final attack of the war.

- Father Thomas O'Reilly refused to leave his Church of the Immaculate Conception when ordered by Federal authorities in November 1864, just before Sherman ordered the city to be burned. Aware that he might have an issue with many of his own devoutly Catholic men, Sherman gave orders that O'Reilly could stay, and that the area immediately around his church was to be spared. The church survived the war with little damage, but was devastated in a fire in 1982.

- WSB had the first "official" motto of any broadcast station in the United States, "Welcome South, Brother."

- WSB opened an FM station at 104.5 (later 98.5) in 1944, and the station gained one of the first television licenses issued by the Federal Communications Commission (FCC) on January 8, 1948. The news that WSB had a television transmission license made a sensation in the city; 2,500 relatively expensive television sets were sold *before* the station actually went on the air on September 13, 1948!

- The creator of the popular 1970s TV series, *WKRP in Cincinnati,* Hugh Wilson, had previously worked in the advertising industry in Atlanta and had friends at WQXI, then one of the most popular local radio stations. Allegedly, he based much of the TV series on the wacky personalities and antics there, and two of *WKRP's* most popular episodes, the "turkey drop" disaster and the "dancing ducks" episode, were specifically based on actual, very similar promotions done by Jerry Blum at WQXI. Bill Dial, the writer of the "turkey drop" episode and an occasional actor on the show, also had an Atlanta radio connection; he had previously worked at both WSB and WAKE before taking up writing and producing.

- The Cathys were Varsity customers in the 1940s, the family having moved into the nearby Techwood Homes the year they opened. Fourteen-year-old Truett Cathy was a frequent customer and greatly impressed with the quality and speed of Gordy's operation. He later credited Gordy with much of his early success when he started his own fast food empire, Chick-fil-A.

- Aged veterans of the Civil War were often addressed by ranks far exceeding their wartime station as a tribute to their cherished status. This is why there are so many "Generals," "Colonels," and "Captains" seen in pictures of them in the early twentieth century.

- There were exactly 2,031 tickets available for the premiere of *Gone with the Wind,* at Loew's Grand Theater, on December 15, 1939. Each ticket cost $10.00, the equivalent of $153.00 today.

- The famous painting of Scarlett O'Hara featured in the movie *Gone with the Wind* was later offered by the studio to the High Museum of Art in Atlanta. It was rejected because "it wasn't art."

- In February 1987, just a month after the civil rights marches and only six months after her program went on the air, talk show host Oprah Winfrey came to Forsyth County to discuss the racial issues and divisiveness that had made national news. She was visibly surprised to find out that most of the county residents in her audience favored racial integration, and later remarked that this was one of her favorite shows.

- Georgia Tech operated a small nuclear reactor right in the heart of the city for many years, closing it just before the 1996 Olympics.

- Atlanta had under 5 million residents, but over 3.5 million Facebook users, as of January 2011. Fifty-seven percent of those users were female.

- Though located in a state in the Deep South, Atlanta has a surprisingly wide range of temperatures during the year. Records range from -5 to 105 degrees in the city. It also snows an average of a little over two inches each winter. It has, however, only snowed three times on Christmas Day in its history, most recently in 2010.

- The Georgia State Capitol building was covered in 1959 with forty-three ounces of nearly pure gold mined in Dahlonega, Georgia. In 1981 it was regilded with sixty ounces of gold, again from Dahlonega. Both times the gold was milled down to the thickness of the tinfoil around a stick of chewing gum.

- Franklin Garrett, the only official historian of Atlanta and author of *Atlanta & Environs,* hosted a trivia night at the Atlanta Historical Society for many years entitled "Stump Franklin." He was stumped just once, over the price of a ticket on an obscure and short-lived streetcar line. Many other attempts were made over the years to trip him up; on one occasion, he was asked the name of the doorman at the downtown Davidson's department store in the 1920s. His reply was, "Which door?"

- The old Atlanta-Fulton County Stadium had the highest altitude of any baseball or football stadium when it opened in 1965. It gained the nickname, "the launching pad," for the high number of home runs hit there, including Hank Aaron's historic 715th home run in 1974. The former site of the stadium is now a parking lot for adjacent Turner Field.

- Grady Memorial Hospital in southwest Atlanta is the largest hospital in Georgia. The main public hospital for the Atlanta metro area, it is one of only four Level I Trauma Centers in Georgia, and the only one within one hundred miles of the city. It has its own Emergency Medical Service that responds to over one hundred twenty thousand calls a year; the very high volume of violent trauma victims transported by GEMS and treated in the Grady ER's have given them the nickname of the "Knife and Gun Club." Some of the finest and most innovative paramedics and EMTs in the world have worked for GEMS, which first began transporting patients in horse-drawn ambulances in 1892.

BIBLIOGRAPHY

The "Pitch-Tree" (1814)

"Buckhead History," WWW Buckhead Incorporated. www
.buckhead.net/history/fort-peachtree/index.html.

White, Max E., Ph.D. *Georgia's Indian Heritage: The Prehistoric
Peoples and Historic Tribes of Georgia.* Roswell, GA: WH Wolfe
Associates, 1988.

Terminus Becomes Marthasville (1843)

"Creation of the Western and Atlantic Railroad." *About North
Georgia.* http://ngeorgia.com/railroads/warr01.html.

Felton, Rebecca Latimer. *Country Life in Georgia in the Days of My
Youth.* Chapel Hill: University of North Carolina Press, 1997.

Johnston, James Houstoun. *Western and Atlantic Railroad of the
State of Georgia.* Atlanta: Georgia Public Service Commission
Publication, 1931.

Winn, Les R. *Ghost Trains & Depots of Georgia: 1833–1933.*
Chamblee, GA: Big Shanty Publishing Co., 1995.

The Battle of East Atlanta (1864)

Castel, Albert. *Decision in the West: The Atlanta Campaign of 1864.*
Lawrence: University of Kansas Press, 1992.

Gabel, Christopher R. *Railroad Generalship: Foundations of Civil War Strategy.* U.S. Army Command and General Staff College, Combat Studies Institute, 1997.

Garrett, Franklin M., ed. "Atlanta in the Civil War," *The Atlanta Historical Journal,* Summer 1979, Vol. 23, No. 2.

McKay, John. *Brave Men in Desperate Times: The Lives of Civil War Soldiers.* Helena, MT: TwoDot, 2007.

Sherman Burns Atlanta (1864)

Hoehling, A. A. *Last Train from Atlanta.* Harrisburg, PA: Stackpole Books, 1992.

McKay, John. *The Insiders' Guide to Civil War Sites in the Southern States.* Helena, MT: Falcon Publishing, 2000.

The Founding of Atlanta University (1865)

Bacote, Clarence A. *The Story of Atlanta University: A Century of Service, 1865–1965.* Atlanta, GA: Atlanta University, 1969.

Clowney, Earle D. "Clark Atlanta University," *New Georgia Encyclopedia.* www.georgiaencyclopedia.org.

The Freedmen's Bureau Online. http://freedmensbureau.com.

Jones, James Pickett. *Yankee Blitzkrieg: Wilson's Raid through Alabama and Georgia.* Athens: University of Georgia Press, 1987.

Morris Rich Opens His General Store (1867)

Bailey, Matthew. "Rich's Department Store," *New Georgia Encyclopedia.* www.georgiaencyclopedia.org.

Sibley, Celestine. *Dear Store: An Affectionate Portrait of Rich's.* Garden City, NY: Doubleday, 1967.

The Invention of Coca-Cola (1886)

Allen, Frederick. *Secret Formula.* New York, NY: Harper Business, 1994.

The Cotton States and International Exposition (1895)

Davis, Harold. *Henry Grady's New South: Atlanta, a Brave Beautiful City.* Tuscaloosa: University of Alabama Press, 1990.

The Official Catalogue of the Cotton States and International Exposition: Atlanta, Georgia, U.S.A., September 18 to December 31, 1895, Illustrated. Atlanta: Claflin & Mellichamp, Publishers, 1895.

Perdue, Theda. *Race and the Atlanta Cotton States Exposition of 1895.* Athens: University of Georgia Press, 2010.

Race Riots and Auburn Avenue (1906)

Bauerlein, Mark. *Negrophobia: A Race Riot in Atlanta, 1906.* New York: Encounter Books, 2002.

Burns, Rebecca. *Rage in the Gate City: The Story of the 1906 Atlanta Race Riot.* Cincinnati, OH: Emmis Books, 2006.

Mixon, Gregory, and Clifford Kuhn. "Atlanta Race Riot of 1906," *New Georgia Encyclopedia.* www.georgiaencyclopedia.org.

The First Flight in Atlanta (1910)

"Airport History." Hartsfield-Jackson Atlanta International Airport. www.atlanta-airport.com/sublevels/airport_info/histpage.htm.

Braden, Betsy, and Paul Hagen. *A Dream Takes Flight: Hartsfield Atlanta International Airport and Aviation in Atlanta.* Athens: University of Georgia Press, 1989.

Hudson, Paul Stephen. "Ben Epps (1888–1937)," *New Georgia Encyclopedia.* www.georgiaencyclopedia.org.

The Met Arrives in Atlanta (1910)

Cason, Caroline. "Atlanta Opera," *New Georgia Encyclopedia*. www
.georgiaencyclopedia.org.

Gough, Peggy M. "Entertainment in Atlanta: 1860–1870."
Master's thesis, University of California, Santa Barbara, 1977.

The Lynching of Leo Frank (1913)

Dinnerstein, Leonard. *The Leo Frank Case*. Athens: The University
of Georgia Press, 1987.

Hertzberg, Steven. *Strangers within the Gate City: The Jews of
Atlanta, 1845–1915*. Philadelphia: Jewish Publication Society of
America, 1978

Oney, Steve. *And the Dead Shall Rise: The Murder of Mary Phagan
and the Lynching of Leo Frank*. New York: Pantheon Books,
2003.

The Klan Reborn (1915)

Freeman, David. *Carved in Stone: The History of Stone Mountain*.
Macon, GA: Mercer University Press, 1997.

Lay, Shawn. "Ku Klux Klan in the Twentieth Century," *New
Georgia Encyclopedia*. www.georgiaencyclopedia.org.

Trelease, Allen W. *White Terror: The Ku Klux Klan Conspiracy
and Southern Reconstruction*. Baton Rouge: Louisiana State
University Press, 1995.

Cumberland versus Georgia Tech (1916)

Bowers, Matt. "Georgia Tech Football," *New Georgia Encyclopedia*.
www.georgiaencyclopedia.org.

Cromartie, Bill. *Clean Old-Fashioned Hate*. Huntsville, AL: Strode
Publishers, 1977.

"The Game of the Century." Cumberland University website. www2.cumberland.edu/about/gotc/index.html.

Paul, Jim. *You Dropped It, You Pick It Up.* Baton Rouge, LA: Ed's Publishing Company, 1983.

WSB Radio's First Broadcast (1922)

Archer, Gleason. *History of Radio to 1926.* New York: Stratford Press, 1938.

Cox Broadcasting Company. *Welcome South, Brother: 50 Years of Broadcasting at WSB, Atlanta.* Atlanta: Cox Broadcasting, 1974.

Lewis, Tom. *Empire of the Air: The Men Who Made Radio.* New York: Perennial, 1993.

White, Thomas. "United States Early Radio History," *Early Radio History.* http://earlyradiohistory.us.

Frank Gordy Opens the Varsity (1928)

Edge, John T. *Southern Belly: The Ultimate Food Lover's Companion to the South.* New York: Algonquin, 2007.

Parker, Dick. *What'll Ya Have: A History of The Varsity.* Decatur, GA: Looking Glass Books, 2003.

The Premiere of *Gone with the Wind* (1939)

Bridges, Herb. *Gone with the Wind: The Three-Day Premiere in Atlanta.* Macon, GA: Mercer University Press, 1999.

Edwards, Anne. *The Road to Tara: The Life of Margaret Mitchell.* New Haven, CT: Ticknor & Fields, 1983.

Harmetz, Aljean. *On the Road to Tara: The Making of Gone with the Wind.* New York: Abrams, 1996.

The Band of Brothers Marches through Atlanta (1943)

Ambrose, Stephen. *Band of Brothers: E Company, 506th Regiment, 101st Airborne from Normandy to Hitler's Eagles Nest.* New York: Simon & Schuster, 1993.

Cole, Hugh M. *The United States Army in World War II: The European Theater of Operations: The Ardennes: Battle of the Bulge.* Washington, DC: U.S. Government Printing Office, 1965.

Crater, Paul. *Images of America: World War II in Atlanta.* Charleston, SC: Arcadia Publishing, 2003.

Griffith, Joe. "The Story of Camp Toccoa: Running for Those Famed Silver Wings," *North Georgia Journal,* Summer 2000, pp. 10–18.

"Toccoa History," 506th Airborne Infantry Regiment Association (Airmobile-Air Assault). www.506infantry.org.

The Deadliest Hotel Fire (1946)

———. *Holocaust on Peachtree: The Story of the Winecoff Hotel.* Atlanta Fire Department, manuscript compiled for the Atlanta Historical Society, July 7, 1969.

Campbell, Steve B. *Prompt to Action: Atlanta Fire Department, 1860–1960.* Atlanta, GA: Atlanta Fire Department, 1960.

Heys, Sam. *The Winecoff Fire: The Untold Story of America's Deadliest Hotel Fire.* Atlanta: Longstreet Press, 1993.

The Temple Bombing (1958)

Branch, Taylor. *Parting the Waters: America in the King Years, 1954–63.* New York: Simon & Schuster, 1988.

———. *Pillar of Fire: America in the King Years, 1963–1965.* New York: Simon & Schuster, 1998.

Greene, Melissa Fay. *The Temple Bombing.* Reading, MA: Addison-Wesley Publishing Company, 1996.

Stoner, J. B. *J. B. Stoner: Televised Political Commercials, 1972–1990.* Norman, Oklahoma: Julian P. Kanter Political Commercial Archive at the University of Oklahoma. www.ou.edu/pccenter/PCC_Update_09/PCC_Home.html.

Webb, Clive. "Counterblast: How the Atlanta Temple Bombing Strengthened the Civil Rights Cause," *Southern Spaces,* June 22, 2009. http://southernspaces.org/2009/counterblast-how-atlanta-temple-bombing-strengthened-civil-rights-cause.

Lenox Square Mall Opens (1959)

Craig, Robert M. "Shopping Center Architecture," *New Georgia Encyclopedia.* www.georgiaencyclopedia.org.

"Lenox Square Mall," *Sky City: Southern Retail Then and Now.* http://skycity2.blogspot.com.

Mitchell, Wright. "Lenox Square site once was the home of great joy," *Buckhead Reporter.* www.reporternewspapers.net.

Martin Luther King Jr.'s Funeral (1968)

Branch, Taylor. *At Canaan's Edge: America in the King Years 1965–68.* New York: Simon & Schuster, 2006.

Burns, Rebecca. *Burial for a King: Martin Luther King Jr.'s Funeral and the Week that Transformed Atlanta and Rocked the Nation.* New York: Scribner, 2011.

Jacobs, Hal. "Lester! The Strange but True Tale of Georgia's Unlikeliest Governor." *Creative Loafing,* March 20, 1999.

Posner, Gerald L. *Killing the Dream: James Earl Ray and the Assassination of Martin Luther King, Jr.* New York: Random House, 1998.

Ice Storm (1973)

"Ice Storms," *Storm Encyclopedia.* The Weather Channel. www
.weather.com/encyclopedia/winter/ice.html.

The Atlanta Child Murders (1979–1981)

"Atlanta Child Murders," Federal Bureau of Investigation, FOIA
documents 1a-9b, 2,825 pages. http://foia.fbi.gov/foiaindex/
atlanta.htm.

Baldwin, James. *The Evidence of Things Not Seen.* Cutchogue, NY:
Buccaneer Books, 1995.

Dettlinger, Chet. *The List.* Atlanta, GA: Philmay Enterprises, 1983.

Douglas, John, and Mark Olshaker. *Mind Hunter: Inside the FBI's
Elite Serial Crime Unit.* New York: Pocket Star Books, 1996.

Jenkins, James S. *Murder in Atlanta: Sensational Crimes that Rocked
the Nation.* Atlanta, GA: Cherokee Publishing, 1981.

Mallard, Jack. *The Atlanta Child Murders: The Night Stalker.*
Charleston, SC: BookSurge Publishing, 2009.

Polk, Jim. "DNA test strengthens Atlanta child killings case,"
CNN Justice, June 9, 2010. http://articles.cnn.com/2010-06-09/
justice/williams.dna.test_1_hair-samples-dna-testing-harold-
deadman?_s=PM:CRIME.

The Limelight Disco Opens (1980)

Echols, Alice. *Hot Stuff: Disco and the Remaking of American
Culture.* New York: W. W. Norton, 2010.

Jones, Alan, and Jussi Kantonen. *Saturday Night Forever: The Story
of Disco.* Chicago: A Cappella Books, 1999.

Shapiro, Peter. *Turn the Beat Around: The Secret History of Disco.*
New York: Faber and Faber, 2005.

Waterhouse, Jon. "Ghosts of hotspots past," *Creative Loafing.* http://clatl.com/atlanta/ghosts-of-hotspots-past/ Content?oid=1241280.

Hosea Williams Marches in Forsyth County (1987)

Bagley, Garland C. *History of Forsyth County, Georgia, Vol. 2.* Easley, SC: Southern Historical Press, 1990.

"Forsyth County Civil Rights March, January, 1987," *About North Georgia.* http://ngeorgia.com/ang/Civil_Rights_March,_ January,_1987.

Huff, Christopher Allen. "Forsyth County," *New Georgia Encyclopedia.* http://www.georgiaencyclopedia.org.

James E. McKinney v. Southern White Knights, Knights of the Ku Klux Klan. 1:87-cv-565-CAM (1988).

Jaspin, Elliot. *Buried in the Bitter Waters: The Hidden History of Racial Cleansing in America.* New York: Basic Books, 2007.

"White Protestors Disrupt 'Walk For Brotherhood' In Georgia Town," *New York Times,* January 18, 1987. www.nytimes .com/1987/01/18/us/white-protestors-disrupt-walk-for-brotherhood-in-georgia-town.html.

Muhammad Ali Lights the Olympic Torch (1996)

"Atlanta 1996 Summer Olympics," Olympic.org. www.olympic .org/atlanta-1996-summer-olympics.

Baker, S Zebulon. "Whatwuzit?: The 1996 Atlanta Summer Olympics Reconsidered," *Southern Spaces,* March 21, 2006. http://southernspaces.org/2006/whatwuzit-1996-atlanta-summer-olympics-reconsidered.

Aerial Rescue at the Atlanta Mill Fire (1999)

Denny, Ken. "Mysteries: Atlanta's Fire Equipment—Found," *Barnards Atlanta Photographs.* www.denneymedia.com/atlanta1864/fire/fire.htm.

Rhodes, J. David, and Matt Moseley. "Atlanta Mill Fire and Helicopter Rescue," *Fire Engineering,* June 1, 1999, Vol. 152. No. 6. http://www.fireengineering.com/index/articles/generic-article-tools-template.articles.fire-engineering.volume-152.issue-6.features.atlanta-mill-fire-and-helicopter-rescue.html.

The Ghosts in the Lab (2001)

Henderson, Donald A., et al. "Smallpox as a Biological Weapon: Medical and Public Health Management," *Journal of the American Medical Association,* June 9, 1999, Vol. 281, No. 22, pp. 2127–2137.

LeDuc, James, et al. "Smallpox Research Activities: U.S. Interagency Collaboration, 2001," *CDC Emerging Infectious Diseases,* Vol. 8, No. 7, July 2002. www.cdc.gov/ncidod/eid/vol8no7/02-0032.htm.

Malkin, Michelle. "The forgotten jihadists in Georgia," MichelleMalkin.com. January 15, 2008. http://michellemalkin.com/2008/01/15/the-forgotten-jihadists-in-georgia.

Preston, Richard. *The Demon in the Freezer.* New York: Random House, 2002.

Tucker, Jonathan B. *Scourge: The Once and Future Threat of Smallpox.* New York: Grove Press, 2002.

The First Atlanta Tornado (2008)

"2008 Atlanta Tornado,"About North Georgia. http://ngeorgia.com/ang/2008_Atlanta_Tornado.

"2008 Atlanta tornado outbreak," Wikipedia.com. http://en
.wikipedia.org/wiki/2008_Atlanta_tornado_outbreak.

"Atlanta Tornado," *The Weather Channel: Storm Stories.* http://
stormstories.weather.com/shows/atlanta-tornado.php.

"Atlanta Tornado, 14 March 2008," Event Record, National
Climatic Data Center, National Oceanic and Atmospheric
Administration. www4.ncdc.noaa.gov/cgi-win/wwcgi
.dll?wwevent-ShowEvent-697463.

"U.S. Tornado Climatology," National Climatic Data Center,
National Oceanic and Atmospheric Administration. www.ncdc
.noaa.gov/oa/climate/severeweather/tornadoes.html.

Wessels, Chris, and Steven P. Woodworth. "Atlanta Tornado;
Fulton Cotton Mill Lofts Search Operations," *Fire Engineering.*
June 1, 2008, Vol. 161, No. 6, pp. 79+.

Atlanta Facts and Trivia

Kassel, Michael. *America's Favorite Radio Station: WKRP in
Cincinnati.* Madison, WI: Popular Press, 1993.

GENERAL SOURCES

Newspapers

Atlanta Constitution
Atlanta Georgian
Atlanta Intelligencer
Atlanta Journal

Books and Periodicals

Allen, Frederick. *Atlanta Rising: The Invention of an International
City, 1946–1996.* Atlanta, GA: Longstreet Press, 1996.

Buffington, Perry, and Kim Underwood. *Archival Atlanta*. Atlanta, GA: Peachtree Publishers, 1996.

Garrett, Franklin. *Atlanta and Environs: A Chronicle of Its People and Events, Volumes I & II*. Athens: University of Georgia Press, 1954.

———. *Yesterday's Atlanta*. Atlanta: Cherokee Publishing, 1994.

Garrison, Webb. *The Legacy of Atlanta: A Short History*. Atlanta, GA: Peachtree Publishers, 1987.

Lankevich, George, ed. *Atlanta: A Chronological & Documentary History, 1813–1976*. Dobbs Ferry, NY: Oceana Publications, 1978.

Leckie, George. *Georgia: A Guide to Its Towns and Countryside* (WPA Guides Series). Atlanta: Georgia Dept. of Education, 1940.

Martin, Harold. *Atlanta and Environs: A Chronicle of Its People and Events: Years of Change and Challenge, 1940–1976, Volume III*. Athens: The University of Georgia Press, 1987

McKay, John, and Bonnie McKay. *The Insiders' Guide to Atlanta*. Guilford, CT: Globe Pequot Press, 2004.

Roth, Darlene R., and Andy Ambrose. *Metropolitan Frontiers: A Short History of Atlanta*. Atlanta, GA: Longstreet Press, 1996.

Russell, James. *Atlanta 1847–1890: City Building in the Old South and the New*. Baton Rouge: Louisiana State University Press, 1988.

INDEX

INDEX

ABOUT THE AUTHOR

John McKay is a near-native of Atlanta, growing up in the Brookhaven area near Buckhead and Lenox Square, and rarely leaving the area since. He is a historian specializing in military subjects, especially the Western Theater of the American Civil War, and a high school history and government teacher. He is a veteran of the U.S. Army and Georgia Army National Guard, worked for many years as a paramedic and firefighter in and around Atlanta, and lives in the northern suburbs with his wife, Bonnie, a nurse, professionally trained chef, and recovering debutante.